UNCOVERING
JACK THE RIPPER'S
LONDON

UNCOVERING
JACK THE RIPPER'S
LONDON

RICHARD JONES

PHOTOGRAPHY BY SEAN EAST

NEW
HOLLAND

First published 2013 by
New Holland Publishers Pty Ltd
London • Sydney • Cape Town • Auckland

Garfield House 86–88 Edgware Road London W2 2EA United Kingdom
Wembley Square First Floor Solan Road Gardens Cape Town 8001 South Africa
1/66 Gibbes Street Chatswood NSW 2067 Australia
218 Lake Road Northcote Auckland New Zealand

www.newhollandpublishers.com

A record of this book is held at the British Library AND/OR National Library of Australia

ISBN 9781780095073

Publisher: Fiona Schultz
Publishing manager: Jo Hemmings
Project editor: Gareth Jones
Copy editor: Gill Harvey
Designer: Lorena Susak
Cartographer: William Smuts
Indexer: Cathy Heath
Production director: Olga Dementiev
Printer: Toppan Leefung Printing Limited

10 9 8 7 6 5 4 3 2 1

Keep up with New Holland Publishers on Facebook http://www.facebook.com/NewHollandPublishers

PREVIOUS: The Ten Bells Pub, Commercial Street, E16.

OPPOSITE: Hanbury Street, at its junction with Wilkes Street.

CONTENTS

PREFACE

In the autumn of 1888 a series of brutal murders in the East End of London sent shock waves reverberating around the civilized world and caused a scandal that struck right at the heart of the British establishment. Officially, the killer was never caught, but thanks to the signature on a letter that was sent to a news agency he became known as 'Jack the Ripper', a name that would catapult him into the realm of legend.

This book is not about hunting him down and naming him. Rather, it is the story of the historical and social background against which the murders occurred; the story of the living conditions in a certain section of East London, where conditions were so horrific that many people at the time viewed the unknown killer as a creature spawned by the area's slums. It is the story of the hardworking Jewish immigrants, who had fled in ever increasing numbers from persecution in Eastern Europe, only to find themselves the victims of hostile elements within the press, which, in seeking to blame them for the murders, almost sparked a pogrom in the East End of London. But above all else it is the story of 12 weeks in 1888, when an unknown killer stalked the shadows of only a tiny section of the Victorian metropolis, yet had an impact that was felt throughout the world.

This account is for all those who have an interest in Jack the Ripper and want to know the story behind the murders. I have endeavored to portray the effect of the murders on the people who lived in the area through contemporary newspaper accounts and reports compiled by philanthropic bodies, which used the murders to try and bring about a reform of the horrific social conditions. I have also attempted to give an idea of the problems faced by the police as they hunted the killer in one of London's most densely populated and criminally active districts.

What I have not tried to do is name Jack the Ripper. There is no doubt that several of the police officers who worked on the case were convinced that they knew the killer's identity; some of them even went on record to name him. The problem is that most of them named different suspects. Therein lies the difficulty of hunting him down: with hundreds of suspects to choose from, attempting the exercise can simply create more confusion. I have detailed the suspects who were arrested, as I feel that these give an insight into how the police operated, what type of person they thought they were looking for, and just how many lunatics were loose in the streets of the East End at the time.

Although no one can say for certain exactly how many victims there were, it is generally agreed that there were five and that the time frame for the murders lasted only from August 31st to November 9th, 1888. This book concentrates on that period, since all the press coverage and official reports provide us with an unrivaled insight into that time. At the height of the Jack the Ripper scare, journalists from all over the world headed to London to experience first hand the streets and alleys where the murders were taking place. They have left us with a series of fascinating tableaux, which enable us to view the East End streets of 1888 and experience something of the panic and hopelessness that engulfed the district during the so-called 'autumn of terror'. To me this is far more interesting than any attempt to solve the mystery could ever be.

I hope you enjoy the book and that it provides you with a true insight into that autumn long ago, when the whole of London literally walked in terror.

Richard Jones
www.rippertour.com

1 Former Commercial Street Police Station

2 Mary Kelly's murder site (former Dorset Street)

3 Annie Chapman's murder site

4 Mary Nichol's murder site

5 Former Working Lads' Institute

6 Site of attack on Emma Smith

7 Martha Tabram's murder site

8 Catherine Eddowes' murder site

9 Former Leman Street Police Station

10 Elizabeth Stride's murder site (former Berner Street)

THE BITTER CRY OF OUTCAST LONDON

In London there is an East End and a West End. In the West End are those fortunate ones who are sent into the world with a kiss. In the East End are the others. Here live the poor, the shamed, those whom Fate, seeing how shrunken and bent they are as they creep through the gates of life, spat in their face for good measure. In this East End a corner has been set aside where, not content with the spittle, Fate sends the poor on their way with a blow, a kick, and their hats shoved over their eyes. In this spot, with the holy name Whitechapel... we would have to sink or swim, survive or go under, find bread, or if we could not, find death.
Jacob Adler (1855-1926)

On June 21st, 1887, Queen Victoria celebrated 50 'glorious' years as monarch, and her subjects marked the occasion with feasting and public ceremonies. The middle classes had particular cause to celebrate, since the past half century had seen them rise to become masters of industry, finance, and international trade. Fortunes were there for the making and the taking, and the middle classes embraced the philosophy of unencumbered self-enrichment with a vengeance. The British Empire was ever expanding, and core British values such as justice, truth, and harmony were being exported throughout Africa, the

Middle East, and Asia. The City of London, the financial boilerroom that powered the Empire and its expansion, reflected the supreme confidence of the age, and the majority of its workers enjoyed reasonable affluence, while increasing numbers of them led lifestyles of wealth and privilege. Yet beneath this façade there lay a general feeling of unease. By the 1880s, the ordered society that had come to be viewed as a birthright by the middle and upper classes was under threat like never before. Many were casting nervous glances toward the East End where a huge underclass of dispossessed and displaced citizenry was beginning to bare its teeth and demand a fair share of the profits, benefits, and spoils of the Empire.

LEFT: Even Queen Victoria took an interest in the Jack the Ripper murders and, at the height of the scare, called for her government to take 'decided action'.

RIGHT: Many of the middle class citizens of Victorian London walked in daily fear that the downtrodden poor would one day rise up in revolution.

The term 'East End', used to describe the area that lay beyond the City of London's eastern fringe, was in fact an invention of the early 1880s. But it soon caught on and was enthusiastically embraced by the popular press, which used it to create a universal image of the area as a hotbed of villainy and degradation. As Robert Sinclair, in his book East London, put it:

> A shabby man from Paddingtn, St Marylebone or Battersea might pass muster as one of the rspectable poor. But the same man coming from Bethnal Green, Shadwell or Wapping was an 'East Ender'; the box of Keeting's bug powder must be reached for, and the spoons locked up... it became a concentrated reminder to the public conscience that nothing to be found in the East End should be tolerated in a Christian country.

In 1883 the Reverend Andrew Mearns had shocked the delicate sensibilities of the English middle classes with The Bitter Cry Of Outcast London: An Inquiry into the Condition of the Abject Poor. This comparatively small publication confronted the bourgeoisie with the grim reality of everyday life in London's slums, and warned that they ignored the festering underclass that dwelt in them at their peril:

> Whilst we have been building our churches and solacing ourselves with our religion and dreaming that the millennium was coming, the poor have been growing poorer, the wretched more miserable, and the immoral more corrupt; the gulf has been daily widening which separates the lowest classes of our community from our churches and chapels, and from all decency and civilisation... how can those places [in which they live] be called homes... To get into them you have to penetrate courts reeking with poisonous and malodorous gases arising from the accumulations of sewage and refuse scattered in all directions and often flowing beneath your feet... walls and ceilings are black with the accretions of filth which have gathered upon them through years of neglect. It is exuding through cracks in the boards overhead; it is running down the walls. It is everywhere... Where there are beds they are simply heaps of dirty rags, shavings or straw, but for the most part these miserable beings find rest only upon the filthy boards...

Although the Victorian metropolis had many slum areas, it was on those of the East End that public attention began to focus. Whitechapel had the capital's worst slums, its worst overcrowding, and the highest death rates. One of its least salubrious neighborhoods lay to the west and east of Commercial

Street. Here the dregs of Victorian society were crammed into 'common lodging houses', many of which were breeding grounds for crime and vice. Inspector Walter Dew, a local detective who began his career at Commercial Street Police Station in 1887, would later write in his memoirs that 'even before the advent of Jack the Ripper [the district] had a reputation for vice and villainy unequalled anywhere else in the British Isles'.

In addition, the area was the place of last resort for huge numbers of homeless drifters, who, on failing to find shelter behind the decaying walls of a common lodging house, would either tramp the streets all night long or else attempt to sleep in the corners of dark passageways and on the landings and stairwells of tenement buildings. Sometimes they would even seek out the stairs or entrance halls of those houses where the anti-social hours worked by the lodgers necessitated the front doors being left open throughout the night.

The conditions in the East End had largely been brought about as a result of the authorities turning a blind eye to the poverty and dreadful overcrowding that were endemic there. Even when they tried to appease their critics by appearing to do something, their measures were often woefully inadequate.

In 1875 Parliament passed the Artisans and Labourers Dwelling Act, to 'allow and to encourage… the purchase and demolition… of large areas of unfit property'. The proximity of Whitechapel and Spitalfields to the wealthier parts of London, coupled with the alarming fact that 80 per cent of the poor were living in 'unfit' properties, ensured that the district was one of the first to be earmarked for demolition and regeneration. Thus the slum clearances began and almost immediately ran into the problem of philanthropy versus blatant profiteering.

Parliament was emphatic that the work of redevelopment would not be financed from the public purse. The onus therefore fell on the private sector, with the necessary incentive being a return on investment that, quite evidently, was not going to be generated by building houses for the poor. Thus the rents for the new model dwellings, which began to appear about the streets of Spitalfields and Whitechapel, were well beyond the means of the people that the government had intended them for. These indigenous poor were forced into an ever decreasing number of slum houses and common lodging houses where the laws of supply and demand ensured that huge numbers of men, women, and children were crammed together, allowing their landlords, who could also look

LEFT: This view shows Whitechapel High Street as it was. In the distance is the spire of St Mary's Church. This was once a lime-washed building and thus became the 'White chapel' that gave its name to the district.

forward to compensation for lost rents when their properties were eventually demolished, to wring as much profit as possible from their misfortune.

The plight of the area's poor had been further highlighted in May 1887 when Charles Booth, a wealthy shipping magnate and successful businessman turned philanthropist, presented a paper to the Royal Statistical Society outlining the grim reality for many who lived in the East End. Out of a population of 456,877 people, he estimated that 22 per cent were living on the poverty line, while 13 percent were struggling against conditions in which 'decent life was not imaginable'. Put simply, 60,000 East End men, women, and children lived their daily lives on the brink of starvation, crammed into overcrowded accommodation where disease, hunger, neglect, and even violence would claim the lives of one in four children before they reached the age of five.

Some social commentators were well aware of the consequences that could ensue should this trampled underclass be pushed beyond endurance and decide to fight back. In her book, *In Darkest London*, Margaret Harkness, writing under the pseudonym John Law, warned: 'The whole of the East End is starving. The West End is bad, or mad, not to see that if things go on like this we must have a revolution. One fine day the people about here will go desperate, and they will walk westwards, cutting throats and hurling brickbats, until they are shot down by the military…'

Fear of the huge underclass that dwelt beyond the City of London's eastern boundary had reached a crescendo by 1888. Many West End citizens were casting nervous glances eastward, fearful that a revolution was inevitable. Jack the Ripper arrived on the scene at just the right moment and came to personify all the nebulous fears and prejudices that the middle and upper classes shared about the East End. As a result, the murders had an impact on society as a whole, and ensured that for several months in 1888 an international spotlight was turned on the conditions that many believed had given birth to this monster of the slums.

BELOW: Food stalls on the streets of the East End were commonplace in an age when refrigeration was unknown.

CHAPTER ONE

THE PEOPLE OF THE ABYSS

The people who lived in the East End comprised a cross section of the lower strata of Victorian society. The 19th century had seen a steady flow of economic migrants drifting into London from other parts of the country. Essex, which had been decimated by the decline of its cloth and farming industries and was one of the poorest counties in England, had seen a huge migration of its surplus poor to East London.

Irish immigrants had also started arriving with the potato famines of 1845 and later. Many of these were reluctant immigrants, who had not wanted to end up amid the squalor of East London, but had found themselves marooned there when their attempts to find ultimate redemption in America had failed. They settled into areas around the riverside, the majority of them finding work on the docks.

But by far the largest immigration into the East End had been that of Jews who had been arriving in increasing numbers from 1881 onwards, fleeing persecution or economic hardship in Russia, Poland, and Germany. By 1888 the Jewish population of Whitechapel had grown to 45,000–50,000. At first these Jewish immigrants had settled in streets to the south of Spitalfields, but by 1888 they had begun expanding into other parts of the East End. Charles Booth recorded how:

> The newcomers have gradually replaced the English population in whole districts... Formerly in Whitechapel, Commercial Street roughly divided the Jewish haunts of Petticoat Lane and Goulston Street from the rougher English quarter lying in the East [this would have been the area of Wentworth Street and Brick Lane]. Now the Jews have flowed across the line; Hanbury Street, Fashion Street, Pelham Street, Booth Street, Old Montague Street, and many streets and lanes and alleys have fallen before them; they fill whole blocks of model dwellings; they have introduced new trades as well as new habits and they live and crowd together and work and meet their fate independent of the great stream of London life surging around them.

As the decade wore on and an economic depression saw the spectre of mass unemployment sweep across the East End, attitudes began to harden toward the Jewish immigrants. In February 1886 the *Pall Mall Gazette* had warned its readers that 'the foreign Jews of no nationality whatever are becoming a pest and a menace to the poor native born East Ender'.

By 1888 high local unemployment, combined with an acute housing shortage in the East End, had focused national attention on the immigrant problem, and two select committees were formed to look into it. The first met in the House of Commons between July 27th and August 8th, and focused on alien immigration. The other met in the House of Lords and investigated the so-called 'sweating' system in the East End, whereby employees were crammed into what were often tiny, stinking, and unwholesome workshops to work anything up to 16 hours a day for wages that amounted to little more than a pittance. This was seen as being particularly prevalent amongst the newly arrived Jewish immigrants, or 'greeners', as they were called. Arnold White, imperialist, author, and arch mover in the antialienist campaign told

OPPOSITE: These old houses in Spitalfields have now been gentrified, but in 1888 they formed the backcloth against which the Jack the Ripper saga was played out.

LEFT: There had been a huge immigration of poor foreign Jews into the East End in the 1880s. The difference in their lifestyle and culture make them very unpopular with the gentile populace.

the committee in terms that are still sadly familiar today, albeit in relation to different scapegoats:

The poor Russian Jew laughs at what he hears of English poverty and scanty fare. He has a false notion that the English artisan is generally overfed, and easily discontented, and that the Jew can live easily where an Englishman would starve!

White's prejudices were debunked by several prominent Anglo-Jewish MPs, most notably East End MP Samuel Montagu, but he was reflecting sentiments that, by the middle of 1888, were held by large numbers of East End residents. The committee was also addressed by Charles Freak, secretary of the Shoemaker Society (a trade that was synonymous with Whitechapel), who let loose a vicious piece of xenophobia: 'These Jew foreigners work in our trade at this common work sixteen or eighteen hours a day, and the consequence is that they make a lot of cheap and nasty stuff that destroys the market and injures us'.

He went on to accuse the Jewish immigrants of frustrating English workmen in their battle to attain higher wages by blacklegging during disputes and taking 'work out at any price'.

The immigrants were also criticized by fellow Jews, including Henry de Jonge, an English Jew of Dutch descent, who, despite being retained as Yiddish interpreter and legal adviser for the aliens, felt compelled to enlighten the committee about populist Gentile views and prejudices. Jews had, he claimed, displaced native tradesmen, who were now only able to gain 'a precarious living compared with what they were in the habit of getting'. By way of illustration he explained how 'wages in tailoring, shoemaking, and cabinet making, which had once stood at £2 a week, had now dropped by half to £1 and £1 5s'.

The committees would ultimately vindicate the immigrants, but their prolonged deliberations ensured that the matter was in the public eye throughout the first eight months of 1888. In *Out of Work*, John Law (aka Margaret Harkness) quotes the wife of a radical carpenter, who expresses the sentiments of many in the East End of London: 'Why should they come here I'd like to know? London ain't what it used to be; it's just like a foreign city. The food ain't English; the talk ain't English. Why should all them foreigners come here to take our food out of our mouths, and live on victuals we wouldn't give to pigs?'

A notorious East End murder, in which both the perpetrator and victim had been Jewish, had occurred in June 1887, and had impacted negatively on the Jewish community. Israel Lipski, who was lodging in the attic of 16 Batty Street just off Commercial Road, had forcibly poisoned fellow lodger Miriam Angel with nitric acid. Although Lipski was hanged for the crime, the newspaper reports of it had fuelled a great deal of anti-Semitism and by 1888 'Lipski' had become a term of abuse frequently used by Gentiles to insult Jews.

One fact that went unnoticed, or at least unremarked upon, by the alienists and the more xenophobic elements of the press, was that when Jewish immigrants moved into a neighborhood they tended to have a remarkably civilizing effect on their surroundings. Social workers, reformers, and even the police were quick to observe how an influx of Jews into a particular neighborhood would soon raise the standards and behavior in some of the worst parts of London. Streets and blocks notorious for violence and crime became comparatively well behaved after Jewish families moved in. Drunkenness and domestic violence, for example, which were rife throughout Whitechapel, were almost unheard of within the Jewish community.

However, this was not a view shared by a large number of East End inhabitants. The reaction to the Lipski murder of 1887 and the immigration debate throughout the first half of 1888 was such that, by the end of the summer, a general feeling of mistrust and hostility towards the Jewish community existed in the neighborhood. So when the Whitechapel murders confronted the people of London with a new type of crime, unprecedented in its barbarity, the Gentile population were only too willing to blame the murders on the immigrant community. Spurred on by press xenophobia, they came to the conclusion that an Englishman could not be responsible, and were more than happy to wreak vengeance on the community that had already become their scapegoats for virtually all the other ills that blighted their everyday lives.

LEFT: One of the old houses that has survived in Batty Street, the street in which the infamous 'Lipski' murder occurred in 1887.

CHAPTER TWO

UNFORTUNATES AND LODGING HOUSES

Employment in the area centred on the docks and on industries such as tailoring, shoemaking, and cabinetmaking. Each morning, as many as 600 men might arrive at the dock gates hoping to find a day's work at five pence an hour. When the foreman appeared waving aloft the hungered after labor dockets, fights would break out as men scrambled, kicked, and punched their way to the front to ensure that they were among the fortunate few whose families might have food on their tables that night.

Working conditions in the docks were cruel and harsh, but they paled into insignificance against those in the sweatshops of the East End. Sweated labour or 'sweating' saw thousands of East End men and women working under the most horrendous conditions imaginable. For 16 hours a day, sometimes seven days a week, they endured cramped workrooms and foul, noxious air, as they labored to produce low cost, low quality clothing, shoes, and furniture. Any complaint about their working conditions would mean instant dismissal, since a vast reservoir of poverty-stricken labour was always available to employers.

Many women would take in 'outwork' and would labour away in their rooms or lodgings to produce cigars, cigarettes, cheap jewellery, artificial flowers, or anything that required little skill and could be manufactured quickly. Others might take in laundry or repair clothing.

The wages earned were barely enough to pay rental on one tiny room in a decrepit and unsanitary house. The room might be shared by an entire family of anything from three to 12 people, and in times of hardship it was not uncommon for these families to sublet a corner of their room to a lodger in order to help them pay the rent. Many families couldn't even afford a room and lived instead in the cheap common lodging houses that proliferated throughout the streets of Whitechapel. Here they would share a common kitchen area and sleep in dormitories with the likes of hardened criminals, common street prostitutes, and the mentally unstable.

The harshness of their living conditions served to dehumanize many of those whose lot it was to wallow in the filth and degradation of these slums. Most of the children had lost all innocence by the time they reached their teens, at which stage they were expected to find work and help support their families. As *The Bitter Cry of Outcast London* grimly lectured its readers:

> That people condemned to exist under such conditions take to drink and fall into sin is surely a matter for little surprise… Who can wonder that young girls wander off into a life of immorality, which promises release from such conditions? The vilest practices are looked upon with the most matter-of-fact indifference… Entire courts are filled with thieves, prostitutes and liberated convicts. In one street are 35 houses, 32 of which are known to be brothels. In another district are 43 of these houses, and 428 fallen women and girls, many of them not more than 12 years old.

OPPOSITE: This old house in Princelet Street still has the ambience and feel of the 19th century.

LEFT: Each night, thousands of men, women, and children paid four pence to sleep in dormitory beds in common lodging houses.

To a select few, prostitution offered a means of escape from the grinding poverty. Some of the more fortunate girls could find work in brothels in the West End of London or sometimes in Paris. But for the majority, escape from the area was simply not an option and, in times of extreme economic hardship, when men found it almost impossible to get work, many an East End slum family's survival depended on a wife or daughter prostituting herself on the streets.

General Booth, founder of the Salvation Army, spoke of a 'large standing army' of prostitutes 'whose numbers no one can calculate'. He did, however, state that the 'ordinary figure given for London is 60,000 to 80,000'. Whereas this was probably an exaggerated figure, including as it did those that Booth referred to as 'all habitually unchaste women', the fact remains that many of the women from the East End slums saw prostitution as a means whereby they could earn more in one night than they could in a whole week in a sweatshop.

However, the promise of easy money was an illusion, for the streets soon exacted a terrible price for the 'wages of sin'. As General Booth wrote:

This life induced insanity, rheumatism, consumption and all forms of syphilis. Rheumatism and gout are the commonest of these evils. Some were quite crippled by both - young though they were. Consumption sows its seeds broadcast... We have found girls at midnight who are continually prostrated by haemorrhage yet who have no other way of life open.

In the hospitals it is a known fact that these girls are not treated at all like other cases; they inspire disgust, and are most frequently discharged before being really cured.

Scorned by their relations, and ashamed to make their case known even to those who would help them, unable [any] longer to struggle out on the streets to earn the bread of shame, there are girls lying in many a dark hole in this big city positively rotting away and maintained by their old companions on the streets.

Their clients were made up of a cross section of Victorian society. The nearby docks provided a steady stream of sailors from all over the world who came ashore with money to spend. The hay market on Whitechapel Road and Whitechapel High Street brought in clients from the agricultural provinces. Sons of middle and upper class families were also drawn by the allure of cheap sex that was available on East End streets. The blatant hypocrisy of many of these young men, who were applauded in polite circles for the self-imposed chastity that their later marriages supposedly entailed, attracted the opprobrium of a writer for *Justice* who fumed:

The young men of the middle and upper classes are commended...for being more prudent and provident than those of the working class because they marry late in life; these expounders and eulogisers of the present

RIGHT: Even if a person could afford their own room the living conditions were still atrocious.

system...conveniently ignore that these prudent and provident young men usually gratify their passions by ruining the daughters of the working class, which economic conditions offer as a vicarious sacrifice for the ladies of the wealthy classes to whom these popinjays of society ultimately unite themselves.

Many of the women thus ruined had little choice but to embrace their roles as 'unfortunates' (a Victorian term for very low-class prostitutes) and would attach themselves to a 'bully' or pimp, who would invariably treat them abominably. Domestic violence was commonplace, as was violence from their clients. Yet even the seemingly well-meaning activities of reformers could have an adverse affect upon them.

Throughout the winter of 1887–88 Frederick Charrington, heir to the local brewing dynasty (in fact he had abandoned his right to inherit, but kept the income), was spearheading a determined campaign to rid the East End of vice. He abhorred the number of brothels in the area and used the Criminal Law Amendment Act of 1885 – under which a citizen could report any house suspected of operating as a brothel to the police in return for a reward – to launch his own private crusade to close them down. Armed with a large black book to note down suspect houses, Charrington cut a swathe through the East End flesh trade that saw brothel after brothel close. His biographer, Guy Thorne, observed how 'the bullies [pimps], the keepers of evil houses, the horrible folk who battened on shame, and enriched themselves with the wages of sin, feared Frederick Charrington as they feared no policeman, no inspector, no other living thing'.

His campaign against the 'foulest sinks of iniquity' resulted in at least one startling revelation for Charrington himself. He had learnt that a girl was being kept against her will at a certain brothel, and set out to rescue her in the company of two detectives who were disguised as water inspectors. They quickly gained admittance to the property and the girl was duly saved. But on searching the rest of the house, he was astonished to find a large portrait of himself staring down from the wall of the main reception room. The detectives informed him that every brothel in the East End possessed a similar portrait, as the keepers wished to be able to identify the man who was doing their trade so much harm!

According to Thorne, Charrington's raids resulted in the closure of 200 brothels in the area. But his campaign, however well meaning, had dire consequences for the displaced prostitutes, who had little choice but to move to other areas – thus, as one newspaper correspondent put it, 'spreading the moral contagion' – or else solicit on the streets in all weathers. The latter generated a great deal of criticism in the letter columns of the local newspapers. Charrington was accused of adding to the misfortune of women who had already been 'gravely wronged by men'. His evangelical endeavors would be one of the reasons why so many women were forced to risk their lives on the streets of the East End in the autumn of 1888, since the brothels, however bad the majority might have been, would at least have afforded them some protection from the threat of being butchered by Jack the Ripper.

All Jack the Ripper's victims belonged to this class of unfortunates, and all of them lived in the relatively small neighborhood to the east and west of Commercial Street, on which social reformers had been focusing their attention for several years. A recurrent theme was the necessity to rid the district of the common lodging houses together with their lawless populace. It did not go unnoticed that two of Jack the Ripper's victims, Mary Nichols and Annie Chapman, had effectively been sent to their deaths as a result of being evicted from their lodging houses, because they lacked the four or eight pence needed to pay for their beds. Three of Jack the Ripper's victims had, at one time or another, lived in the same lodging house in Flower and Dean Street, one of a group of local streets known to be the blackest of black, where vice, violence, and villainy flourished.

By law, every one of these common lodging houses had to be licensed and was subject to strict police supervision. Each one had to display a placard in a prominent position stating the number of beds for which it was licensed, a number that was calculated on the basis of a minimum allowance of space per person. Bed linen had to be changed weekly, and the windows had to be thrown open daily at 10am to ensure that the rooms were well ventilated. Men and women's dormitories were supposed to be separate, and rooms for married couples partitioned off. Every lodging house had a common kitchen where the lodgers would gather and cook whatever food they had managed to buy, beg, steal, or scavenge in the course of the day.

Most of the lodging houses were owned by middle-class entrepreneurs and investors, the majority of whom lived well outside the area and entrusted the day-to-day running of the businesses to 'wardens' or 'keepers'. Many of these had criminal backgrounds and operated on the periphery of the law. They would turn a blind eye – probably in return for a share of the proceeds – to illegal activity, and blatantly flouted the regulation, which stated that men and women – unless married – must be kept separate.

In a letter to the *Daily Telegraph* on September 21st, 1888, a correspondent who signed himself 'Ratepayer' highlighted the problem. Referring to Thrawl Street, where Mary Nichols, Jack the Ripper's first victim, was lodging at the time of her murder, he wrote:

> The population is of such a class that robberies and scenes of violence are of common occurrence. It is a risk for any respectable person to venture down the turning even in the open day. Thieves, loose women, and bad characters abound, and, although the police are not subject, perhaps, to quite the same dangers as they were a few years ago, there is still reason to believe that a constable will avoid, as far as he can, this part of his beat, unless accompanied by a brother officer.

His letter also revealed just how numerous the common lodging houses were throughout the relatively small area that was bounded by Baker's Row to the east, Middlesex Street to the west and Whitechapel Road to the south:

> There are no less than 146 registered lodging-houses, with a number of beds exceeding 6,000. Of these 1,150 are

in Flower and Dean-street alone, and nearly 700 in Dorset-street. Some of the houses contain as few as four beds, whilst others have as many as 350. At a few of these men only are received, and at others women only, but in the majority there are what are known as 'double-doss beds'. ...there is little room to doubt the truth of the assertion that when these double beds are let no questions are asked, and the door is opened for the most frightful immorality.

On October 10th, 1888, at the height of the Ripper scare, Henrietta Barnett, wife of the Reverend Barnett of St Jude's Church, Commercial Street, forwarded a petition signed by 4,000 'Women of Whitechapel' to Queen Victoria begging her to prevail upon 'your servants in authority' to close down the common lodging houses. The petition was passed to the Home Office, which asked the police to provide information on East End prostitution, brothels, and the common lodging houses. Based on the observations of the H Division constables, whose beats took in the district to the west and east of Commercial Street, the police set the number of common lodging houses at 233, the number of residents at 8,530, and the number of brothels at 62. The police reply also stated that 'we have no means of ascertaining what women are prostitutes and who are not, but there is an impression that there are about 1200 prostitutes, mostly of a very low condition'.

The sheer number of women forced to prostitute themselves on the streets ensured that Jack the Ripper had little difficulty in finding victims. Furthermore, the fact that those women would go with him into pitch-black courtyards, alleys, and passageways made it a simple matter for him to kill them and then melt away into the night without been seen. Either by choice or luck, Jack the Ripper had settled upon the perfect area in which to carry out his murderous reign of terror.

BELOW: Daily life in the common lodging houses tended to focus on the kitchen, where the residents met to cook any morsels they had begged, stolen, or sometimes bought.

CHAPTER THREE

On the Trail of Jack the Ripper

The Jack the Ripper murders were predominantly investigated by the Metropolitan Police. Their headquarters were at 4 Whitehall Place and their commissioner was Sir Charles Warren, who had been appointed to the post in January 1886. In the century and more since the murders occurred, Warren has been subjected to a barrage of largely undeserved criticism and ridicule, most of which is based on several misconceptions and outright inaccuracies about his handling of the case. An ex-military man, he took up office with high hopes of bringing much needed discipline to the Metropolitan Police, and appears to have won the respect and loyalty of most of the rank and file officers. *The Times* applauded him as being '…precisely the man whom sensible Londoners would have chosen to preside over the Police Force of the Metropolis…there are few officials…who have had more varied experience. He is at once a man of science and a man of action'.

Warren's reputation as a man of action was put to the test on November 13th, 1887, a day that became known as 'Bloody Sunday'. During the summer of 1887 large numbers of destitute unemployed had begun camping out in Trafalgar Square and using it as a meeting place. As a result the square had become a hotbed of political agitation, and Warren, fearing that this growing disquiet might soon place London at the mercy of the mob, requested that the Home Secretary, Henry Matthews, ban all meetings there. Matthews, a typical career politician, prevaricated for almost two months, forcing Warren to send 2,000 policemen into the square at weekends to maintain public order. In early November, Matthews finally made a decision, and Warren was authorized to veto further meetings. Up until that point, the left-wing press had looked upon Warren as an intellectual progressive and had afforded him a reasonable amount of respect. But they saw the ban as his personal doing and, feeling it to be unlawful, the Metropolitan Radical Association decided to challenge it by calling a meeting in Trafalgar Square for 2:30 pm on Sunday November 13th. Warren stuck to his guns and expressly forbade any procession from entering the square at the appointed time.

The stage was set for confrontation and, according to newspaper reports, 20,000 protestors (the police estimated twice that number, the organizers half) converged on the square. Warren had stationed 2,000 constables, two deep, in a ring around the square's interior, and a further 3,000 were kept in readiness, along with a battalion of Grenadier Guard foot soldiers and a regiment of mounted Life Guards. The three leaders of the Social Democratic Federation – Hyndman, Burns, and Cunninghame Graham – linked arms and vowed to breach the circle. Hyndman was lost in the crowd, but the other two made it to the police line, exchanged blows with the officers and were duly arrested and locked up. An idea of the brutality of what was to come can be gleaned from an eye-witness account of the arrest of Cunninghame Grahame, Radical-Socialist MP for Lanark:

After Mr Grahame's arrest was complete one policeman after another, two certainly, but I think no more, stepped up from behind and struck him on the head… with a violence and brutality which were shocking to behold.

OPPOSITE On November 13th, 1887, Metropolitan Police Commissioner Sir Charles Warren had an estimated 20,000 protesters forcibly cleared from Trafalgar Square. So brutally did his men do this that the day became known as 'Bloody Sunday'.

Suddenly the mood of the crowd, which up until that moment had been good humoured, changed. Warren called for reinforcements; 400 foot soldiers and mounted police divisions were deployed to disperse the crowd. Socialist poet Edward Carpenter was in the square and witnessed the carnage that followed.

> The order had gone forth that we were to be kept moving. To keep a crowd moving is, I believe, a technical term for the process of riding roughshod in all directions, scattering, frightening and batoning the people...

Socialist artist Walter Crane, who was also present, commented that, 'I never saw anything more like real warfare in my life'. As the encounter ended, one protestor lay dead (some reports claimed two), 100 people had been hospitalized, 77 constables had been injured, and 40 protestors arrested. By the end of the week, 75 charges of brutality had been lodged against the police.

But as far as the authorities were concerned, Warren was the hero of the hour and had made a decisive stand against both the mob and the threat posed to public order by socialism. *The Times* was fulsome in its praise and commented on how Warren's decisive action had undermined 'a deliberate attempt... to terrorize London by placing the control of the streets in the hands of the criminal classes'.

To the radicals, however, he was now an autocrat, and from that point on they sought any opportunity to attack and undermine him. Consequently, when the Jack the Ripper murders occurred and the police appeared unable to catch the killer, the radical press saw an opportunity to avenge itself on Warren, and he would find himself vilified in many newspapers for his mishandling of the investigation.

Warren may not have been the bungling Colonel Blimp portrayed by many commentators, but he certainly had a fiery temper as well as decidedly fixed ideas about who should have ultimate control over his police force. This made it difficult for him to assume the role of subordinate, which in turn brought him into confrontation with his superior, the Home Secretary, Henry Matthews. Ultimately one of these confrontations would lead to him resigning his post at the height of the Ripper scare.

LEFT: Chief Inspector Donald Swanson was the desk police officer who read and assessed virtually all of the information on the Jack the Ripper Case.

Before the Whitechapel murders began, Warren's assistant commissioner in charge of the Criminal Investigation Department was James Monro. In addition, Monro was in charge of the Metropolitan Police's Secret Department, known as Section D. Section D was directly responsible to the Home Secretary, not the Metropolitan Police Commissioner, leaving Warren in the untenable position of having a subordinate officer with duties beyond his authority or influence. In November 1887, Monro complained to Warren that he was overworked, and suggested that a new post, that of Assistant Chief Constable, be created to relieve the strain he was under. Warren, perhaps understandably, suggested that Monro give up his Section D duties. Relations between the two men deteriorated at an alarming rate over the next seven months, and by August 1888 Monro had tendered his resignation.

Monro's resignation became effective as of August 31st, 1888, coincidentally the date of what is now considered the first Jack the Ripper murder – that of Mary Nichols. His replacement was Dr. Robert Anderson, a Dublin-born lawyer who had been brought to London in 1876 as part of an intelligence branch to combat the threat of Fenian terrorism. When the branch was closed, Anderson had remained behind as a Home Office adviser in matters relating to political crime. By 1888 he had become secretary of the prison commissioners and gladly accepted the post of Assistant Commissioner of the CID when it was offered to him in August 1888. As such he became the highest ranking officer with direct involvement on the Jack the Ripper case.

However, Anderson came to his post suffering from exhaustion, and his doctor instructed that he take a recuperative break. Anderson's chair at Scotland Yard was barely warm when, on September 8th, the day of the second Jack the Ripper murder, he left London for Switzerland, effectively leaving the detective department of the Metropolitan Police leaderless at a time when they were facing the biggest challenge in their history.

Warren was away on holiday himself during the first week of September. On his return he evidently realized that if the hunt for the killer was to succeed, one man had to take sole charge of the investigation. 'I am convinced that the Whitechapel murder case…can be successfully grappled with if it is systematically taken in hand', he dictated in a memo to the Home Office on September 15th. 'I go so far as to say that I could myself unravel the mystery provided I could spare the time & give individual attention to it. I feel therefore the utmost importance to be attached to putting the whole Central Office work in this case in the hands of one man who will have nothing else to concern himself with.'

The man chosen was Chief Inspector Donald Sutherland Swanson, whom one contemporary described as being 'one of the best class of officers'. According to Warren's instructions, Swanson was to be given his own office and 'every paper, every document, every report, every telegram must pass through his hands. He must be consulted on every subject…'

As the officer with overall responsibility for the case (at least until Anderson's return from holiday in early October, after which he was the desk officer under Anderson) Swanson read and assessed all the information to do with the crimes, and as such gained an unrivalled knowledge of the Jack the Ripper murders.

Swanson, Anderson, and Warren were, however, based in Whitehall. The murders, with one exception, were East End affairs; on the ground, the investigation into the killings was handled by two divisions of the Metropolitan Police. The investigation into the murder of Mary Nichols was carried out by officers of J Division, among them Inspectors Spratling and Helson. Those of Annie Chapman, Elizabeth Stride, and Mary Kelly came within the jurisdiction of H Division, the head of which was Superintendent Thomas Arnold – although he too was absent on leave at the time of the first two Jack the Ripper murders, his post being filled by Acting Superintendent West. In charge of the Criminal Investigation Department of

H Division was Inspector Edmund Reid, 'one of the most remarkable men of the century' as the *Weekly Despatch* described him.

It was decided early on in the case, however, that the local detective force would benefit from the involvement of experienced officers from Scotland Yard, and Inspectors Moore, Abberline, and Andrews were duly sent to the district. The senior officer of the three was Inspector Abberline, and he was placed in overall charge of the investigation on the ground.

Inspector Frederick George Abberline was 45 years old in 1888, a portly and balding officer who wore a thick moustache and bushy side whiskers. He had already spent 14 years as a detective with H Division and had gained an unrivalled knowledge of the area's streets and criminals. The satirical magazine *Toby* praised him as 'a well known East Ender…[to whom] scores of persons are indebted… He has a decent amount of curiosity, and has been known to stop gentlemen at the most unholy times and places and enquire about their health and work – questions which are often settled by a magistrate, generally in Mr Abberline's favour.'

The previous year Abberline's dedication and service had been recognized with a promotion to central

office at Scotland Yard, and a farewell dinner was held for him in December 1887 at the Unicorn Tavern, on Shoreditch High Street. But he had barely settled in to his new position when it was decided that his knowledge of East End villains was just what was needed in the hunt for the Whitechapel murderer, and so in early September 1888 he found himself recalled to his old stomping ground of Spitalfields and Whitechapel.

Another officer whose name is worth a brief mention is Sergeant William Thicke, who spent virtually all of his police career with H Division. Walter Dew remembered him as 'a holy terror to the local lawbreakers' and mentioned that the nickname 'Johnny Upright' had been bestowed upon him 'because he was upright both in his walk and in his methods'. His knowledge of the district certainly impressed those newspaper reporters who met him, as did his striking check suits and blond moustache. Thicke appears to have played an important part in the hunt for the murderer; the press reported his presence at the scene of the crime directly after several of the murders.

One other police force investigated the Jack the Ripper murders. The killing of Catherine Eddowes

LEFT: The City Police head-quarters were based in a courtyard tucked away in Old Jewry, a short distance from the Bank of England. It was the City Police who investigated the murder of Catherine Eddowes.

in Mitre Square occurred within the City of London, the financial Square Mile. This meant that her murder came within the jurisdiction of the City of London Police. In charge at the time was Acting Commissioner Major Henry Smith, a popular chief who received a far better press than Sir Charles Warren, largely because the men of his force appeared to show more willingness than the Metropolitan Police to talk to journalists.

The head of the City Police's detective department was Inspector James McWilliam, whose principle talent lay in investigating complex financial fraud. Following the murder of Catherine Eddowes, McWilliam liaised with Chief Inspector Swanson on a daily basis; but his report to the Home Office on the murder, although long and drawn out, contained so little actual information that Home Secretary Henry Matthews was moved to scrawl a note remarking, 'They evidently want to tell us nothing'.

There were, of course, hundreds of police officers on the Jack the Ripper case. But these are the ones whose names will crop up time and again in the pages that follow, and several of them, such as Abberline and Swanson, would in their own way come to know more about the murders than anyone else. However, all of them, in the autumn of 1888, would find themselves pitting their wits against a seemingly new breed of criminal, and many found themselves vilified by the press and public for their apparent inability to catch him.

BELOW: Commercial Street Police Station where many of the officers who investigated the murders were based. The building has now been converted into a block of flats.

CHAPTER FOUR

WITHOUT THE SLIGHTEST TRACE

It is generally accepted today that Jack the Ripper had five victims. But the Whitechapel murders file, in which the Jack the Ripper murders are included, has several other murders on it. Two of these occurred before the murder of Mary Nichols on August 31st, 1888, and several others took place after the murder of Mary Kelly on November 9th, 1888, which, it is generally agreed, were the Ripper's first and final crimes respectively.

However, it is rare for a serial killer to embark suddenly upon a killing spree. There is often a pattern that graduates from attacks and assaults to full-blown murder, wherein a distinctive *modus operandi* is established. Therefore it is highly probable that Jack the Ripper committed other crimes before the murders of his five acknowledged victims.

The newspapers of the time had realized that murderous attacks made good copy and went out of their way to bring their readers the salacious details of many violent and sometimes fatal attacks that occurred in the East End in the months leading up to the Jack the Ripper murders. What becomes apparent, when trawling through the many column inches dedicated to crime in the area, is just how widespread such assaults were. Attacks on women were disturbingly commonplace, and several of these bore the possible hallmarks of Jack the Ripper's work.

On Saturday February 25th, 1888 a 38-year-old widow named Annie Millwood of White's Row, Spitalfields, was admitted to the Whitechapel Workhouse Infirmary suffering from stab wounds to her legs and the lower part of her abdomen. According to the April 7th edition of the *East London Post and City Chronicle* Annie Millwood:

> ...stated that she had been attacked by a man who she did not know, and who stabbed her with a clasp knife which he took from his pocket. No one appears to have seen the attack, and as far as at present is ascertained there is only the woman's statement to bear out the allegations of an attack, though that she had been stabbed cannot be denied. After her admission to the infirmary deceased progressed favourably, and was sent to the South Grove Workhouse, but while engaged in some occupation at the rear of the building she was observed to fall, and on assistance being given it was found that she was dead.

At her subsequent inquest it was apparent that her death was not related to the injuries she had sustained in the assault, and the jury returned a verdict of death from natural causes. That does not, however, preclude her from being an early victim of Jack the Ripper. Her attacker had targeted her lower abdominal region, as would happen in the vicious attack upon Martha Tabram (see page 37), and as would also occur with three of the later victims. The problem is that the information concerning the attack on Annie Millwood is sparse: what we do know of it is based solely on her account of what happened which, it has been suggested, may have been a fiction intended to conceal the fact that her injuries were self-inflicted.

OPPOSITE: It was at the Working Lads Institute on Whitechapel Road that Coroner Wynne Baxter presided over the inquest into the deaths of several of Jack the Ripper's victims.

ABOVE: Emma Smith was attacked here in Osborne Street in the early hours of April 3rd, 1888.

Just over a month later, another attack on a woman was reported by the newspapers. A little after midnight on March 28th, 1888, 39-year-old dressmaker Ada Wilson was sitting in her room at 9 Maidman Street, Mile End, when she heard a knock on the door. Opening it, she found a man aged about 30 standing outside. He was approximately 5 feet 6 inches in height, had a fair moustache and a sunburnt face, and was wearing a dark coat, light trousers, and a wide-awake hat. The man threatened to kill her if she didn't give him money. When Ada refused, he took out a clasp knife and stabbed her twice in the throat. Her screams disturbed her upstairs neighbour, Rose Bierman, who came down to investigate and discovered Ada in a state of near collapse in the hallway.

'Stop that man for cutting my throat', Ada shouted, as a 'fair young man' rushed to the front door, unlocked it, and disappeared into the street.

'I don't know what kind of wound Mrs Wilson received', Rose Bierman later told the Eastern Post, 'but it must have been deep, I should say, from the quantity of blood in the passage'.

Despite a newspaper report that Ada Wilson was in a 'dangerous condition' and it was 'thought impossible she can recover', she did, in fact, make a full recovery and was able to tell the police what had occurred, as well as provide them with a description of her would-be murderer. Whether that man later became Jack the Ripper is open to debate. Some argue that the attack occurred too far east of his

LEFT: George Yard (now Gunthorpe Street) in 1890. It was along this cobbled thoroughfare that Martha Tabram walked with her killer in the early hours of August 7th, 1888.

acknowledged murder sites for there to be a connection. But then is it not equally possible for the killer to have explored different neighbourhoods, until he settled on one where the maze-like complexity of the alleys and passageways made for an easy and unobserved escape from the scenes of his crimes? Others argue that the motive for the attack on Ada Wilson was quite clearly robbery and that Jack the Ripper was not interested in stealing from his victims. It should, however, be remembered that we have only Ada Wilson's testimony that robbery was the motive and, given the fact that she was almost certainly a working prostitute who, according to her neighbor, Rose Bierman, 'often had visitors to see her', it is likely that she was attacked by one of her clients. She may well have invented the demand for cash in an attempt to keep her prostitution secret.

Her attack, however, did share certain similarities with those of Jack the Ripper. She was probably a prostitute: Jack the Ripper would later exclusively target prostitutes. The description of her attacker resembles some later descriptions given by witnesses who may have seen the Ripper with his victims. Ada's assailant not only used a knife, but also targetted her throat: once again, as Jack the Ripper did. Given these similarities, it is possible that the violent assault on Ada Wilson was an early Ripper attack, carried out before he progressed to the horrific mutilations that were the hallmark of his later crimes.

It was a month later, in April 1888, that attitudes began to change. In the early hours of the morning on April 3rd, 1888, a prostitute named Emma Smith was viciously attacked by a gang at the Wentworth Street junction of Osborne Street, the 'dirty, narrow entrance to Brick Lane' according to John Henry Mackay in the *Anarchist*, written in 1891. They robbed her of all the money she had, subjected her to a savage beating, and violently thrust a blunt object into her vagina. As with Ada Wilson and Annie Millwood, Emma Smith survived her initial attack and even managed to stagger back to her nearby lodging house at 18

LEFT: Gunthorpe Street still has a sinister air about it. It was through this archway that 'Pearly Poll' watched Martha Tabarm lead a soldier shortly before her body was discovered at the opposite end of what was then George Yard.

George Street. Here several of her fellow lodgers became alarmed by her bleeding face, cut ear, and evident distress. They persuaded her to go with them to the London Hospital on Whitechapel Road. Unfortunately, although Emma was able to give the doctor who attended her a detailed account of what had happened, peritonitis soon set in and she died at 9 am on April 4th.

The first the police knew of the murder was on April 6th when they were informed by the coroner's office that an inquest into Emma Smith's death was to be held the next day. At that inquest Chief Inspector West, of the Metropolitan Police's H Division, stated that he had no official information on the subject and was only aware of the case 'through the daily papers'. He had, he said, questioned the constables on the beat, but none of them appeared to be any wiser than he was. The coroner, Mr Wynne E. Baxter, decreed that the woman had been 'barbarously murdered' and opined that it was 'impossible to imagine a more brutal and dastardly assault'. The jury willingly followed his suggestion that they should bring in an immediate verdict of 'wilful murder against some person or persons unknown'.

Emma Smith was probably not a victim of Jack the Ripper. Indeed, the fact that she told the attending doctor about a group of men suggests she was attacked by one of the so-called 'High-Rip' gangs that preyed on the district's prostitutes. This was evidently the conclusion that the police came to, and this belief influenced their line of enquiry in the early days of the hunt for Jack the Ripper. But the death of Emma Smith was significant in one major respect. It was with her killing that the police opened their file on the Whitechapel murders, a file that would, by the end of that year, encompass the crimes that have passed into history as the Jack the Ripper murders.

On the bank holiday Monday of August 6th, 1888, Martha Tabram, a local prostitute in her late thirties, went soliciting on Whitechapel Road with Mary Ann Connolly, a very masculine-looking prostitute who was better known in the area as 'Pearly Poll'. They met with two guardsmen, a corporal and a private, and went drinking with them in several pubs along the Whitechapel Road. At some stage between 11:30 pm and 11:45 pm, the group split into couples. A quick round of bargaining took place, prices were agreed and Martha disappeared with her client through the sinister arch that led into George Yard (today known as Gunthorpe Street), while Pearly Poll led her client into the next dark thoroughfare along, Angel Alley.

According to the *East London Advertiser*, George Yard was 'one of the most dangerous streets in the locality'. But for a seasoned streetwalker like Martha Tabram, it offered a reasonable amount of privacy for quick sex acts which were known as 'fourpenny knee tremblers'. Toward the top of George Yard, on the left, there stood a block of cheap apartments, known as George Yard Buildings. According to the East *London Observer*, its tenants were 'people of the poorest description'. When its staircase lights had been extinguished at 11 pm, the landings were cast into an impenetrable darkness that made them ideal for use by prostitutes and their clients. Martha would no doubt have been well aware of this tucked-away spot, and it was for one of the building's dark and secluded landings that she headed with the soldier – and possibly again with a later client.

In the early hours of the morning, Mrs Hewitt, wife of Francis Hewitt, the building's super-intendent, thought she heard a single cry of 'Murder!' She paid it little heed: domestic violence was so common in the area that she and her husband heard such cries on an almost nightly basis, and had long since given up paying them any attention.

At around 2 am, Mrs Elizabeth Mahony and her husband came home to George Yard Buildings, having been out with some friends to celebrate the bank holiday. She went out again afterwards to buy some supper at a chandler's shop in nearby Thrawl Street. She was back within 10 minutes and noticed nothing untoward or suspicious as she ascended the staircase – although she later admitted that the stairs were unlit, so she probably wouldn't have noticed a body if one had been lying there. Once in bed she and her husband slept soundly and heard no noise in the night.

At 3:30 am Alfred George Crow, a cab driver of 35 George Yard Buildings, returned home from work and, on his way upstairs, saw somebody lying on the first floor landing. It was, however, quite common for people to sleep on the building's landings, and so he thought nothing of it and continued home to bed.

A little after 5 am, John Saunders Reeves, a waterside labourer, left his home in George Yard Buildings and came down the stairs. He too noticed the prone form, but as it was now getting light, he was able to see that it was a woman who was lying on her back in a pool of blood. He hurried off to find a policeman and returned with Constable T. Barrett, whom he had encountered patrolling in the vicinity of George Yard. Barrett sent Reeves for local medic Dr. Killeen, who, having carried out an examination of the woman, pronounced life extinct and gave it as his opinion that she had been brutally murdered.

The attack on Martha Tabram had been a frenzied one. There were 39 stab wounds, pepper-potting her body from the throat to her lower abdomen. Dr. Killeen later told the inquest that the killer had used two different blades, the majority of the wounds having been inflicted with an ordinary pocket knife, while a deep wound to her breast had been dealt by 'some long, strong instrument…[which could

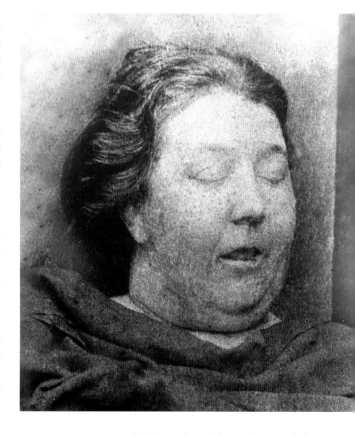

RIGHT: There is still a great deal of debate as to whether or not Martha Tabram was a victim of Jack the Ripper.

have been]…a sword bayonet or dagger'. Significantly he was also of the belief that sexual intercourse had not recently occurred, thus ruling out rape as a motive for the murder.

The viciousness of the killing, coupled with the fact that it had been carried out without anyone hearing a sound, was the subject of considerable puzzlement and disquiet around the area in the days and weeks that followed. *The East London Advertiser* commented:

> The circumstances of this awful tragedy are not only surrounded with the deepest mystery, but there is also a feeling of insecurity to think that in a great city like London, the streets of which are continually patrolled by police, a woman could be foully and horribly killed almost next to the citizens peacefully sleeping in their beds, without a trace or clue being left of the villain who did the deed. There appears to be not the slightest trace of the murderer, and no clue has at present been found.

George Collier, the deputy coroner for the district, would later express the feelings of many who lived in the area when he called the crime 'one of the most dreadful murders any one could imagine', and said of the perpetrator, 'The man must have been a perfect savage to inflict such a number of wounds on a defenceless woman in such a way'.

Today there is considerable debate as to whether or not Martha Tabram was a victim of Jack the Ripper. The investigating officers at the time certainly seem to have believed so. Inspector Walter Dew, who had been transferred to the Metropolitan Police's H Division in 1887 and was one of the detectives who worked on the case, later stated in his autobiography: 'Whatever may be said about the death of Emma Smith, there can be no doubt that the August Bank Holiday murder, which took place in George Yard Buildings…was the handiwork of the dread Ripper…'

The truth is that with the passage of more than a hundred years and the disappearance of so much of the police evidence, the only thing we can say for certain about the Jack the Ripper murders is that nothing is certain.

On the face of it, Martha Tabram's injuries were not consistent with the mutilations sustained by the later victims, who are now generally considered to be and are often referred to as the five 'canonical' victims of Jack the Ripper. Yet, significantly, her killer had targetted Martha's throat and lower abdomen. It is therefore possible, and the word possible requires great emphasis, that Martha Tabram, murdered in the early hours of August 7th, 1888 on the dark, first floor landing of George Yard Buildings, was the first victim to die at the hands of Jack the Ripper.

However, the significance of Martha's murder cannot be underestimated, for it began to impress upon the minds of the police, the press, and the public at large that something decidedly untoward was occurring in Whitechapel, and a wave of general unease began to ripple through the district.

Thus, when only three weeks later, the mutilated body of another prostitute was discovered a little less than half a mile away from George Yard, the realization began to dawn – prematurely, as it transpired – that a repeat killer was on the loose. For the people of London, their autumn of terror was about to begin.

OPPOSITE: Martha and her murderer would probably have passed this building in George Yard. In 1888 it was a refuge for homeless women.

CHAPTER FIVE

Murder of a Most Atrocious Character

At around 3:40 am on August 31st, 1888, a carter named Charles Cross was making his way to work along Buck's Row – a narrow, cobbled Whitechapel street that was lined on one side by dark, imposing warehouse buildings and on the other by a row of two-floor houses. As Cross approached the looming bulk of the 1876 Board School that dominated (and still dominates) the western end of the street, he noticed a dark bundle lying in a gateway on the left. As in so many of the district's thoroughfares, street lighting in Bucks Row was minimal, so at first Cross wasn't sure exactly what it was. It looked a little like a discarded tarpaulin and, thinking that it might prove useful, Cross went over to inspect it. As he drew closer, he realized it was in fact the prone form of a woman.

As Cross stood rooted to the spot, unsure what to do next, he heard footsteps behind him. Turning, he saw another carter, Robert Paul, walking towards him.

'Come and look over here', Cross called. 'There is a woman lying on the pavement.'

The two men stepped gingerly over the road and stooped over her. She was lying on her back, her legs straight out, her skirts raised almost over her waist. Charles Cross reached out and touched her face, which was warm, and her hands, which were cold and limp. 'I believe she is dead', he said.

Robert Paul, meanwhile, placed his hand on the woman's chest, and thought he felt a slight movement. 'I think she's breathing', he said, 'but very little if she is'.

Paul suggested that they sit the woman up, but Cross refused to touch her again. So, because they were late for work and felt they had done as much as they could, they pulled her skirts back down to her knees to recover her decency and set off for their respective places of employment, agreeing to tell the first policeman they encountered of their find. But what neither man had noticed in the pitch darkness of Buck's Row was that the woman's throat had been slashed so savagely that her head had been almost cut from her body.

That discovery was made by beat officer Police Constable John Neil, who turned into Bucks Row and proceeded to walk past the Board School shortly after Cross and Paul had left the scene.

'There was not a soul about', he later told the inquest into the woman's death. 'I had been round there half an hour previously, and saw no one then. I was on the right side…when I noticed a figure lying in the street. It was dark at the time…I examined the body by the aid of my lamp, and noticed blood oozing from a wound in the throat. She was lying on her back, with her clothes disarranged. I felt her arm, which was quite warm from the joints upwards. Her eyes were wide open. Her bonnet was off and lying at her side.'

As Neil bent down over the body, he noticed PC John Thain passing the end of the street and flashed his lantern to attract his attention.

OPPOSITE: The body of Mary Nichols – generally now held to have been the first victim of Jack the Ripper – was discovered here, in the area where the bushes now grow. The Board School is the only building in the immediate vicinity to have survived.

'Here's a woman with her throat cut', he called to his approaching colleague. 'Run at once for Dr. Llewellyn.'

As Thain hurried off to fetch the medic, PC Mizen, who had been alerted by Cross and Paul, arrived at the scene. Neil sent him to bring reinforcements and asked him to fetch the police ambulance.

When Dr. Llewellyn arrived at around 4 am, he carried out a cursory examination of the body and, noting the severity of the wounds to the throat, pronounced life extinct. On closer examination he also observed that the deceased's body and legs were still warm, although her hands and wrists were quite cold. This led him to surmise that she could not have been dead for more than half an hour.

As Llewellyn went about his grim business, news of the murder was beginning to filter through the immediate neighborhood. In adjacent Winthrop Street there stood a horse slaughterers' yard where three slaughtermen – Harry Tomkins, James Mumford, and Charles Britten – had been working throughout the night. They had heard nothing, and knew nothing of the murder until informed of it by PC Thain as he passed their premises *en route* to fetch Dr. Llewellyn. They had gone round to view the body and remained at the scene until the woman was removed to the mortuary. The three men would later find themselves under suspicion and were interrogated separately by the police before being eliminated as suspects.

They were joined at the murder site by Patrick Mulshaw, a night watchman, who was working at the nearby sewer works. Although he confessed that he sometimes dozed on duty, he was emphatic that he had been awake between 3 am and 4 am, and that he had not seen or heard anything suspicious. But around 4:40 am a passing stranger had told him, 'Watchman, old man, I believe somebody is murdered down the street', and he immediately went round to Buck's Row. The police appear to have made attempts to trace Mulshaw's mystery informant, but their enquiries proved unsuccessful.

Dr. Llewellyn was by now becoming a little disconcerted at the number of sightseers arriving at the scene and he ordered that the body be removed to the mortuary where he would make a further examination. Thain and Neil duly lifted the body onto the police ambulance (that was, in reality, little more than a wooden handcart). As they did so, Thain noticed that the back of the woman's clothing was soaked with blood, which he presumed had run down from the neck wound. He also observed a mass of congealed blood underneath the body, which was around 6 inches in diameter and which had begun to run towards the gutter.

The relatively small amount of blood found at the scene, coupled with the fact that no one in the vicinity had heard a sound would, by the end

LEFT: This photograph of Bucks Row shows the houses that once lined it. The murder site was where the garage doors are situated (to the center of the picture).

of the day, lead to speculation that the murder had been carried out elsewhere and the body simply dumped where it was found. As *The Times* informed its readers:

It seemed difficult to believe that the woman received her death wounds there... If the woman was murdered on the spot where the body was found, it is impossible to believe she would not have aroused the neighbourhood by her screams, Bucks-row being a street tenanted all down one side by a respectable class of people...

This theory was given some consideration at the subsequent inquest into the woman's death but the coroner was quick to dismiss it in his summing up:

The condition of the body appeared to prove conclusively that the deceased was killed on the exact spot in which she was found. There was not a trace of blood anywhere, except at the spot where her neck was lying, this circumstance being sufficient to justify the assumption that the injuries to the throat were committed when the woman was on the ground, whilst the state of her clothing and the absence of any blood about her legs suggested that the abdominal injuries were inflicted whilst she was still in the same position.

Evidently most of the blood had been absorbed into the clothing, a fact that was all too apparent to PC Thain, whose hands became covered in the stuff as he lifted her onto the ambulance.

When Inspector Spratling arrived at the scene at around 4:30 am, the body had already been removed and the blood was being washed away by one of the local residents. Spratling headed round to the mortuary in nearby Old Montague Street, which was little more than a brick shed, and there began taking down a description of the deceased. At first he noticed only the neck wounds previously noted by Dr. Llewellyn, but on closer inspection he discovered something that had so far eluded everyone.

Beneath her bloodstained clothing, a deep gash ran all the way along the woman's abdomen. She had been disembowelled.

Spratling sent immediately for Dr. Llwelleyn in order that he might comment on the newly discovered injuries. But before the medic had arrived and could carry out a more detailed inspection, two senile workhouse paupers, Robert Mann and James Hatfield, stripped the body of its clothing and proceeded to wash it down, dumping the garments in an untidy pile in the mortuary yard. The coroner would later criticize the police for allowing this to happen; the police, however, were adamant that they had given instructions that the body was not to be disturbed until Llwelleyn had conducted a full and detailed post mortem examination.

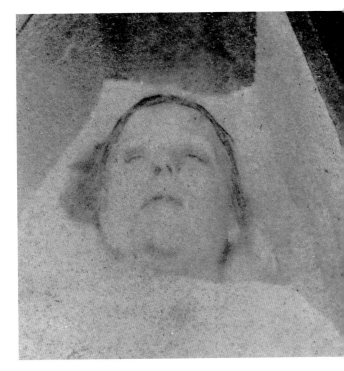

RIGHT: Mary Nichols, the first of the group now known as the 'canonical' victims of Jack the Ripper.

At first the police had no idea who the victim was, so they began canvassing the area in an attempt to discover her identity. Soon several women came forward and identified her as a woman known as 'Polly' who had been living in a nearby lodging house at 18 Thrawl Street. Meanwhile, Inspector Spratling had noticed the mark of the Lambeth Workhouse upon her petticoats, and later that day a resident of the workhouse, Mary Ann Monk, was brought to the mortuary and shown the victim's body. She immediately recognized her as Mary Nichols, a fellow resident up until May 1888.

Mary or 'Polly' Nichols was a 43-year-old prostitute who had begun the morning of her death drinking in the Frying Pan Pub on the corner of Thrawl Street, where she was seen at 12:30 am. From there she had walked along Thrawl Street and, a little the worse for drink, had tried to get a bed in the lodging house at number 18. But she didn't have the required four pence, so the deputy keeper turned her away.

'I'll soon get my doss money', she told him as she left. 'See what a jolly bonnet I'm wearing.' Evidently she intended to resort to prostitution to raise the necessary money and considered that the bonnet would be an irresistible draw to customers. Perhaps she was right, for she seems to have had reasonable success. The last person to see her alive, apart from the murderer, was her good friend Mrs Emily Holland, who met her at 2:30 am outside a grocer's store at the junction of Osborn Street and Whitechapel Road. Mary was obviously drunk and was leaning against the wall. Emily Holland tried to persuade her to return to the lodging house, but Nichols refused, boasting that she had made her lodging house money three times over but had spent it. She was off, she said, to make it one last time.

'It won't be long before I'm back', she told her friend, and staggered off unsteadily.

At some stage in the next hour and a quarter, Mary Nichols would meet her murderer and go with him to the dark gateway toward the top of Buck's Row. There he would suddenly clasp his hand across her mouth, probably asphyxiate her by strangulation, ease her to the ground and cut her throat with a strong-bladed knife. And despite the fact that several people were either sleeping lightly or lying awake in premises that either adjoined or stood opposite the site, none of them would hear a thing or even be aware of the final moments of Polly Nichols: not Mr Purkess, the manager of Essex Wharf, which stood directly across from the murder site on the opposite side of the street; not his wife, who had spent a restless night and who may well have been pacing up and down their bedroom, which looked over at the gateway where the murder had occurred; not Mrs Emma Green, whose bedroom window actually overlooked the murder site and who was, by her own admission a light sleeper, but who had slept on, undisturbed, until awoken by the police after the body had been discovered; not the keeper of the Board School, the towering walls of which still exist (and are all that remain in the vicinity); not even the police constable who had been on duty at the gate of the Great Eastern Railway Yard, some 50 yards from where the body was found.

The killer had committed his crime with ruthless and silent efficiency and then melted, unseen and undetected, into the night. He had probably skirted the Board School into Winthrop Street, and dived down one of the narrow passageways that headed out onto the busy Whitechapel Road. Here he could lose himself in the crowds that thronged it, even at that early hour. As the coroner observed in his summing up at the inquest:

It seems astonishing at first thought that the culprit should have escaped detection, for there must surely have been marks of blood about his person. If, however, blood was principally on his hands, the presence of so many slaughter-houses in the neighbourhood would make the frequenters of this spot familiar with blood-stained clothes and hands, and his appearance might in that way have failed to attract attention while he passed from

Buck's-row in the twilight into Whitechapel-road, and was lost sight of in the morning's market traffic.

As the day progressed, the police continued their investigations throughout the district, desperate for a breakthrough. For the entire day, there appears to have been a general consensus among the police, press, and public that the murder was the work of one of the local gangs, and that the same gang had been responsible for the previous murders of Emma Smith and Martha Tabram. *The Evening News* informed its readers that:

These gangs, who make their appearance during the early hours of the morning, are in the habit of blackmailing these poor unfortunate creatures, and when their demands are refused, violence follows, and in order to avoid their deeds being brought to light they put away their victims. They have been under the observation of the police for some time past, and it is believed that with the prospect of a reward and a free pardon, some of them might be persuaded to turn Queen's evidence, when some startling revelations might be expected.

Meanwhile the police were also busy tracing relatives of the deceased, and had located her father, Edward Walker, and her estranged husband, John Nichols. In the early hours of September 1st, John Nichols was taken to the Old Montague Street Workhouse to view his wife's body. In distress, he shook his head disbelievingly, whispering to her, 'I forgive you, as you are, for what you have been to me'.

BELOW: It was here at the junction of Whitechapel Road and Osborn Street that Mary Nichols was last seen alive by her friend Emily Holland.

CHAPTER SIX

THE HUNT BEGINS

Coroner Wynne Baxter, freshly returned from a holiday in Scandinavia, opened the inquest into the death of Mary Nichols on September 1st, 1888 at the Working Lads' Institute on Whitechapel Road. The newspapers were evidently most impressed by his sartorial elegance; the *East London Observer* commented that he 'appeared at the inquest in a pair of black and white checked trousers, a dazzling white waistcoat, a crimson scarf, and a dark coat'. Coroner Baxter would ultimately preside over the inquests of three Jack the Ripper victims, plus those of two other murder victims who are generally believed to have been killed by someone else. From the outset Baxter demonstrated open hostility towards the police – criticizing them, for example, for not noticing Mary Nichols' abdominal injuries sooner. The inquests would, in fact, become a battle of wills between Coroner Baxter and various police inspectors who, quite naturally, were anxious to keep their lines of enquiry out of the public eye, lest suspects be alerted. Baxter had other ideas, and at times seems to have used the inquests as his own personal sounding board. The result was that they became protracted, drawn-out affairs, thus enabling the newspapers to bring a huge amount of detail to the public and turn the Whitechapel murders into a veritable media circus almost from the outset.

As Baxter's long-winded inquest into the murder of Mary Nichols ground into action, the police began their laborious search for the perpetrator of the crime. They focused their attention on the area of common lodging houses where Nichols, Tabram, and Smith had been staying at the times of their deaths. Officers also began making enquiries among the local prostitutes to see if they could shed any light on the killer's identity. Meanwhile the local people appear to have realized very early on that there was something decidedly different about these killings; crowds began gathering at the murder sites, where they would chat nervously about recent events and air their suspicions about who was responsible. According to the *Daily News*:

> People in the neighbourhood seem very much divided in opinion as to the probability of its being the work of one person or several. The women for the most part appear to incline to the belief that it is a gang that has done this and the other murders, and the shuddering dread of being abroad in the streets after nightfall, expressed by the more nervous of them, is pitiable. 'Thank God! I needn't be out after dark', ejaculated one woman. 'No more needn't I', said another; 'but my two girls have got to come home latish, and I'm all of a fidget till they comes'.

Not everyone, however, was convinced that the crimes were gang related. 'That's a got up yarn', one man told a *Daily News* reporter. 'I rather wish it was true. If there was a gang like that, one or t'other of 'em'd split before long, and it'd all come out. Bet your money this ain't been done that way.'

OPPOSITE: The White Hart still stands alongside Gunthorpe Street as it did in 1888 when Martha Tabram's body was discovered a short distance away.

Meanwhile police enquiries amongst the local prostitutes had yielded a likely sounding suspect, whom the local streetwalkers had nicknamed 'Leather Apron'. Unfortunately they could tell the police very little about him, other than that he habitually wore a leather apron (hence the nickname), that he sometimes wore a deerstalker hat, and that he was running an extortion racket, demanding money off prostitutes and beating up those who refused. Sergeant William Thick was adamant that whenever the people of the area spoke about Leather Apron they were referring to a man named John, or Jack, Pizer. So the police set about trying to find him, to either prove his guilt or eliminate him as a suspect.

Unfortunately, their investigation suffered an almighty setback within days, when, either through the unguarded comments of police officers, or more probably the local tittle-tattle that appears to have been circulating around the lodging houses and hostelries of the district, the newspapers found out about their main suspect. On September 5th the *Star* newspaper ran the first of several articles that alarmed local residents and frustrated the police, who had hoped to keep their suspicions a closely guarded secret:

LEATHER APRON THE ONLY NAME LINKED WITH THE WHITECHAPEL MURDERS. THE STRANGE CHARACTER WHO PROWLS ABOUT AFTER MIDNIGHT. UNIVERSAL FEAR AMONG WOMEN - SLIPPERED FEET AND A SHARP LEATHER-KNIFE.

In two articles the *Star* provided its readers with a description of the character:

He is five feet four or five inches in height and wears a dark close fitting cap. He is thickset, and has an unusually thick neck. His hair is black, and closely clipped, his age being about 38 or 40. He has a small black moustache. The distinguishing feature of his costume is a leather apron, which he always wears, and from which he gets his nickname.

His expression is sinister, and seems to be full of terror for the women who describe it. His eyes are small and glittering. His lips are usually parted in a grin, which is not only not reassuring, but also excessively repellent. He is a slipper maker by trade, but does not work. His business is blackmailing women late at night. A number of men in Whitechapel follow this interesting profession. He has never cut anybody so far as known, but always carries a leather knife, presumably as sharp as leather knives are wont to be. This knife a number of the women have seen. His name nobody knows, but all are united in the belief that he is a Jew or of Jewish parentage, his face being of a marked Hebrew type. But the most singular characteristic of the man, and one which tends to identify him closely with last Friday night's work, is the universal statement that in moving about HE NEVER MAKES ANY NOISE.

What he wears on his feet the women do not know, but they all agree that he moves noiselessly. His uncanny peculiarity to them is that they never see him or know of his presence until he is close by them. When two of the Philpott-street women directed the *Star* reporter to Commercial-street, opposite the Princess Alice Tavern, as the most likely place to find him, she added that it would be necessary to look into all the shadows, as if he was there he would surely be out of sight. This locality, it may be remarked, is but a few steps from the model dwelling house in George's Yard, where the murdered woman of four weeks ago was found.

OPPOSITE: In the early days of the hunt for Jack the Ripper, the prostitutes of the area began to tell the police of a man called 'Leather Apron', who frequented the area around The Princess Alice pub on Commercial Street.

ABOVE: The homeless of Whitechapel used to sleep around the steps and railings of Christ-church, Spitalfields. The Ten Bells pub can be seen on the corner in the background.

The *Star*'s campaign to alert the populace to the noiseless menace in their midst had two effects. The first was that John Pizer learnt of the police's suspicions, and the prospect of falling victim to a baying mob so terrified him that he promptly went into hiding among his relatives.

The second was a far more sinister effect on the neighborhood as a whole, and its repercussions would ultimately influence the way in which the police investigation was handled. The *Star*'s singling out the suspect's Hebrew appearance fed a growing belief amongst the Gentile population that no Englishman could be capable of such brutal and gruesome crimes. Thus anti-Semitism, which had been gaining momentum in the area for several years, began to increasedramatically; the police became alarmed, realizing that it could easily erupt into full-scale anti-Jewish rioting. Such a prospect ensured that later witness statements describing suspects as 'Jewish-looking' would several times be altered by the police to the more universal 'foreign-looking' when disseminated to the public at large. It would also lead the Metropolitan Police Commissioner to order the destruction of a seemingly important clue that directly implicated the Jews in the murders.

Meanwhile the *Star* was stepping up its apparent campaign to terrify the local people. 'THE MAN IS UNQUESTIONABLY MAD', it told its readers on September 6th:

And…anybody who met him face to face would know it… his eyes are never still, but are always shifting uneasily, and he never looks anybody in the eye.

The article also provided a contemporary insight into living conditions in Thrawl Street, where Mary Nichols had been living at the time of her death.

One of our reporters visited one of the single women's lodging-houses last night. It is in Thrawl-street, one of the darkest and most terrible-looking spots in Whitechapel. The house keeps open till one o'clock in the morning, and reopens again at five. In the house nightly are 66 women, who get their bed for 4d. The proprietor of

the place, who is also owner of several other houses of a similar character in the neighbourhood, told some gruesome stories of the man who has now come to be regarded as the terror of the East-end. Night after night, he said, had women come in a fainting condition after being knocked about by 'Leather-Apron'. He himself would never be out in the neighbourhood after twelve o'clock at night except with a loaded revolver. The 'terror', he said, would go to a public house or coffee-room, and peep in through the window to see if a particular woman was there. He would then vanish, lying in wait for his victim at some convenient corner, hidden from the view of everybody.

The police attempted to dampen the rampant speculation by making it known that he was only a suspect. But the *Star* was enjoying its particularly nasty anti-Semitic campaign and reported how:

The hunt for 'Leather Apron' began in earnest last evening (September 5th). Constables 43 and 173, J Division… were detailed to accompany Detective Ewright, of the J Division, in a search through all the quarters where the crazy Jew was likely to be. They began at half-past ten in Church-street, in Shoreditch, rumour having located the suspected man there. They went through lodging-houses, into 'pubs', down side streets, threw their bull's-eyes into every shadow, and searched the quarter thoroughly, but without result.

The effect that the newspapers' demonizing of Leather Apron had on not just the local populace but on the country as a whole is amply illustrated in a highly critical commentary by George Simms for the *Sunday Referee* in mid-September:

It is only the careful observer, the close student of our insular everyday life, the professional expert, who can thoroughly gauge the extent to which Leather Apron has impressed himself upon the public mind. Up to a few days ago the mere mention of Leather Apron's name was sufficient to cause a panic. All England was murmuring his name with bated breath. In one instance, which is duly recorded in the police reports, a man merely went into a public-house and said that he knew Leather Apron, and the customers, leaving their drinks unfinished, fled *en masse*, while the landlady, speechless with terror, bolted out of a back door and ran to the police-station, leaving the grim humourist in sole possession of the establishment, till and all. Never since the days of Burke and Hare has a name borne such fearful significance.

The fact that the police seemed helpless in their endeavours to catch the killer, brought increased criticism from the local residents, several of whom voiced their concerns in angry letters to the newspapers. Mr

Henry T. Tibbatts, of 24 Artillery Lane, Bishopsgate Street wrote to the *Daily News* on September 3rd bemoaning the fact that:

[As an] East end man, having business premises within a stone's throw of Whitechapel Church, [I contend that] our police protection is shamefully [in] adequate, and that the scenes that hourly and daily are enacted in this locality are a disgrace to our vaunted progress. I myself have witnessed street fights amounting almost to murder in the neighbourhood of Osborn street, Fashion street, &c., and never at any of these critical periods are the police to be found. Only within the last few days has a most disgraceful scene been enacted close to my own gates in Spitalfields, but then as ever the police were conspicuous by their absence, and such things are of common occurrence. It is quite time some one spoke out plainly...

In actual fact, several local residents were already endeavouring to bring a sense of order to the area. In the aftermath of Martha Tabram's murder a meeting of about 70 men from the immediate neighborhood of George Yard had been held. Following a brief discussion, 12 men were appointed to act as watchers whose duties were to observe certain streets, chiefly between the hours of 11 pm and 1 am, and not only try to support the action of the police when necessary, but also to take careful note of disorderly houses and the causes of any disturbance. This committee, the St Jude's Vigilance Committee, operated out of Toynbee Hall on Commercial Street, and was the first one of several such vigilance committees to be formed by local residents. In addition to these committees, many men were venturing out onto the streets of Whitechapel and Spitalfields hoping to catch the killer themselves.

'No less a personage than a director of the Bank of England', reported the *Echo*, 'is so possessed by personal conviction that he had disguised himself as a day labourer, and is exploring the public houses, the common lodging houses, and other likely places to find the murderer'.

These vigilance patrols and amateur detectives would ultimately prove more of a bane than a blessing to the police. Ordinary beat officers sometimes found it difficult to distinguish between the indigenous cranks and crackpots that habitually wandered the streets by night and these newcomers – several of whom were, to say the least, decidedly odd. Plain clothes detectives and members of vigilance patrols would shadow a suspicious-looking character about the streets, only to find he was one of these amateur sleuths. In addition, however well meaning they were, the information they provided had the effect of almost overwhelming the police with a deluge of duff leads and bogus suspects. A correspondent to the *St James Gazette* summed up the problems caused to the police by amateur patrols, and warned that the murderer had probably already spotted the opportunities offered by them:

And it is well known to the police, that... the extraordinary proceedings of the amateur detectives who nightly patrol Whitechapel are of great help - to the murderer in evading discovery. Every wrongful arrest and every wild goose chase after the murderer's cousin on which the police are sent tends distinctly in the murderer's favour... And, unfortunately, just at present the police dare not, as they should, tell the amateur detectives to go home... If the murderer be possessed, as I imagine he is, with the usual cunning of lunacy, I should think it probable that he was one of the first to enrol himself among the amateur detectives.

In the wake of Mary Nichols' murder, the police themselves began increasing their patrols in the district. Meanwhile, the local people had little choice but to go about their daily business, mindful that another atrocity was probably inevitable. On September 7th, a journalist on the *East London Advertiser* set about penning his copy for the next day's edition.

If, as we imagine, there be a murderous lunatic concealed in the slums of Whitechapel, who issues forth at night... to prey upon the defenceless women of the 'unfortunate' class, we have little doubt that he will be captured. The cunning of the lunatic, especially of the criminal lunatic, is well-known; but a lunatic of this sort can scarcely remain at large for any length of time in the teeming neighbourhood of Whitechapel. The terror which, since Thursday last, has inspired every man and woman in the district, will keep every eye on the watch. A watch should be kept indeed behind the windows in every street in Whitechapel. The murderer must creep out from somewhere; he must patrol the streets

It was a prophetic piece of journalism. For by the time the first edition of the newspaper was hitting the streets on the morning of September 8th, the people of Whitechapel were already waking up to the news that the killer had struck again.

BELOW: Some of the older parts of Whitechapel still have the ambience of the 1880s and can be quite atmospheric when darkness falls.

CHAPTER SEVEN

'DARK' ANNIE CHAPMAN

Like Mary Nichols, Martha Tabram, and Emma Smith, Annie Chapman led a somewhat nomadic existence around Spitalfields. She was 45 years old, a short, plump, ashen-faced consumptive who for four or so months prior to her death had been living at Crossingham's lodging house at 35 Dorset Street, where she paid eight pence a night for a double bed. She appears to have enjoyed a cordial relationship with the other tenants and the deputy keeper, Timothy Donovan, remembered her as being an inoffensive soul whose main weakness was a fondness for drink. Like many of the women in the area, Annie supplemented the meagre income she obtained from crochet work and making and selling artificial flowers with prostitution. She appears to have had two regular clients, one known as Harry the Hawker, and the other a man named Ted Stanley, a supposed retired soldier who was known to her fellow lodgers as the 'Pensioner'. As it later transpired, Stanley was neither a retired soldier nor a pensioner, but was in fact a bricklayer's labourer who lived at 1 Osborn Place, Whitechapel. According to Timothy Donovan, Stanley frequently spent Saturday to Monday with Annie at Crossingham's. He also claimed that Stanley had told him to turn Annie away should she ever arrive at the lodging house with other men. Stanley vehemently denied this and claimed to have visited Annie only once or twice.

Whatever Annie's relationship with the 'Pensioner', he seems to have been the cause of the only trouble that Timothy Donovan could remember her being involved in during all her time at Crossingham's. At some stage in the month before her death (different witnesses remembered different dates), there had been a fracas between Annie and fellow lodger Eliza Cooper. The full details of the argument as told by the different witnesses are confusing and contradictory, with some even claiming that Harry the Hawker was the cause. According to Eliza Cooper in her inquest testimony, she had loaned Annie Chapman a bar of soap, which Annie had given to Ted Stanley, who then went to wash with it. Over the next few days Eliza asked several times for the return of the soap, only to be dismissed by Annie, who on one occasion contemptuously tossed a ha'penny onto the lodging house kitchen table and told her to 'Go and get a halfpenny of soap'. The animosity was still evident when the two women met a few days later in the Britannia pub on the eastern corner of Dorset Street. However, on this occasion, Annie slapped Eliza across the face, screaming as she did so, 'Think yourself lucky I don't do more'. Eliza retaliated by punching Annie in the eye and then hard across the chest. Annie appears to have come off worse from the exchange of blows, and the bruises she sustained were still evident when Dr. Phillips carried out her post mortem.

As a result, Annie Chapman's last days were spent bruised and in pain, her health rapidly failing. On Monday September 3rd, when she met her friend Amelia Palmer on Dorset Street, the bruising to her right temple was more than evident.

'How did you get that?' Amelia Palmer asked.

Annie's response was to open her dress and show her the bruising on her chest. Amelia saw Annie again

OPPOSITE: Christchurch, Spitalfields still dominates the surrounding area, just as it did in 1888 when the victims of Jack the Ripper, and even, perhaps, the murderer himself, would have gazed upon it on a daily basis.

LEFT: It was here in Hanbury Street that 'Dark' Annie Chapman, the second victim of Jack the Ripper was seen talking to a man shortly before her murder.

the next day close to Spitalfields church and commented on how pale she looked. Annie told her that she felt no better and that she might admit herself to the casual ward for a few days. When Amelia asked if she had had anything to eat that day Annie replied, 'No, I haven't had a cup of tea today'. Amelia handed her twopence so she could buy some food, and warned her not to spend it on rum.

Three days later, at around 5 pm on September 7th, Amelia saw Annie once again in Dorset Street. This time she looked even worse and complained of feeling 'too ill to do anything'. She was still standing in the same place when Amelia passed her again 10 minutes later, although she was now trying desperately to rally her spirits.

'It's no use giving way, I must pull myself together and get some money or I shall have no lodgings', were the last words Amelia Palmer heard Annie Chapman speak.

At around 7 pm, Annie turned up at Crossingham's Lodging House and asked Timothy Donovan if she could sit in the kitchen. Since he hadn't seen her for a number of days, he asked where she had been.

'In the infirmary', she replied.

He allowed her to go to the kitchen where she remained until the early hours of the next morning. Shortly after midnight Donovan sent John Evans to the kitchen to collect the money for her bed. He found her eating potatoes, a little the worse for drink.

When he asked her for the money she wearily replied, 'I haven't got it. I am weak and ill and have been in the infirmary.'

She went up to the office and tried to persuade Donovan to let her stay a little longer.

Donovan told her bluntly, 'You can find money for your beer but you can't find money for your bed'. Shaking his head, he told her that if she couldn't pay, she couldn't stay.

Realizing that further discussion was futile, Annie turned to leave, but as she did so she asked him to save the bed, adding that, 'I shall not be long before I am in'. She stood for a few minutes in the doorway and reiterated her point: 'I shall soon be back, don't let the bed'.

John Davis escorted her off the premises and watched her as she went, observing later that she appeared to be slightly tipsy as opposed to drunk. She headed through Little Paternoster Row, turned right along Brushfield Street, and walked towards the looming, almost sinister, bulk of Spitalfields Church.

'Dark Annie', as she was known locally, was evidently confident that she could quickly earn the money from prostitution, but her movements for the next three or so hours have never been established. Later that day one of the bar staff at the Ten Bells pub, at the junction of Commercial Street and Church Street (today's Fournier Street), told a journalist that a woman answering Annie Chapman's description had been drinking in the pub at around 5 am when a man in a 'little skull cap' popped his head round the door and called her out. The veracity of this sighting is difficult to ascertain. What is certain is that by 5:30 am Annie Chapman had made her way to Hanbury Street, just a short distance away from the Ten Bells.

The four-floor houses that lined Hanbury Street had front doors that opened into narrow passageways, which squeezed past the staircases and led directly to the back yards. The rooms were let out to individual tenants and their families. Since many of them worked all hours of the day and night, the front doors tended to remain open all night long, a fact that didn't go unnoticed by the localprostitutes who frequently led their clients into the back yards of the houses, or even the hallways and landings, for what the coroner at Annie Chapman's inquest described as 'immoral purposes'. Number 29 was typical of the houses on the street, and a total of 17 occupants were crowded into its eight rooms.

At between 4:40 am and 4:45 am John Richardson, son of Amelia Richardson, one of the residents at 29 Hanbury Street who also ran a packing case business from the premises, stopped off at the building on his way to work to check the yard from which his mother operated her business. A few months previously, someone had broken the padlock on the cellar door in the back yard, and ever since he had visited regularly to make sure that nothing was amiss. On this particular morning one of his boots was pinching his toe, so he sat down on the step to trim off some of the leather with a table knife. From where he was sitting he could see that the padlock to the cellar door was intact, and standing up again, he set off for work. He later estimated that he had sat on the step for two or so minutes and had been aware of nothing out of the ordinary.

At some stage between 5:15 am and 5:32 am, Albert Cadoche, a carpenter

RIGHT: Annie Chapman probably led her killer though the door of 29 Hanbury Street, knowing that its backyard would offer some privacy for what was known as a 'fourpenny knee trembler'.

who lived at 27 Hanbury Street, went out into his back yard. As he returned towards the back door he heard a woman's voice say, 'No'. He couldn't be certain exactly where it had come from, but thought it was from the yard of number 29, next door. Cadoche went indoors but returned to the yard three or four minutes later, at which time he heard something fall against the fence that divided the yards of numbers 27 and 29.

'It seemed as if something touched the fence suddenly', he told the inquest.

He did not, however, look over the fence, but instead went back through the house and set off for work along Hanbury Street, then turned left along Commercial Street. Here he looked up at the clock of Christchurch, Spitalfields and saw that it was 5:32 am.

Just after the nearby brewery clock chimed 5:30 am, Mrs Elizabeth Long turned out of Brick Lane and walked along Hanbury Street en route for Spitalfields Market. She noticed a man and a woman talking on the right-hand pavement a little before she reached the door of number 29. She didn't see the man's face, only his back, but she described him as being of foreign appearance with a dark complexion. He looked shabby but genteel, was aged about 40, and was not much more than 5 feet in height. He had on a dark overcoat, and wore a brown deerstalker hat. She got a better view of the woman, because she was facing her; so, when taken to see Annie Chapman's body at the mortuary, she was certain it was her

that she had seen. Mrs Long later told the inquest that the couple 'were talking pretty loudly', and so she overheard the man say in a foreign accent, 'Will you?' To which the woman replied, 'Yes'. But since, as she later told the coroner, it was quite common for her to see couples standing there in the morning, Mrs Long found nothing suspicious about this particular couple and continued on her way.

A little before 6 am, John Davis, an elderly resident of 29 Hanbury Street, came downstairs, walked along the narrow passageway and opened the back door. The sight that met his eyes sent him recoiling in horror. Moments later Henry John Holland, who was walking along Hanbury Street, and James Kent and James Green Hanbury, who were standing in the street, were startled by the sudden appearance of an

LEFT: Elizabeth Long was certain on the time she last saw Annie Chapman because she heard the brewery clock here on Brick Lane chime half-past-five in the morning, as she turned into Hanbury Street.

RIGHT: It was down this staircase that John Davis came at around 6 am on September 8th, 1888. Turning along the passageway, he made a gruesome discovery that sent him reeling out into the street.

agitated old man who came stumbling into the street from the doorway of number 29.

'Men!' he cried. 'Come here.'

Nervously they followed him along the passageway and looking into the yard saw the mutilated body of Annie Chapman lying on the ground between the steps and the wooden fence. Her head was turned towards the house and her clothes had been tugged up above her waist exposing her red and white striped stockings. A handkerchief was tied around her throat (she had been wearing this when the killer cut her throat and it had not, as has often been asserted, been tied by her murderer to 'stop the head from rolling away'). Her face and hands were covered in blood, and her hands were raised and bent with the palms towards the upper portion of her body giving James Kent the impression that she had 'been struggling…[and] had fought for her throat'.

After a few moments of stunned silence, the men sprang into action, raced from the house, and set off in different directions to find a policeman. In the case of James Kent, the horror of what he had witnessed began to sink in immediately, causing him to abandon his search and go instead for a brandy to steady his nerves. Henry Holland raced up to Commercial Street and headed across to Spitalfields Market where he encountered a constable on fixed point duty. Holland panted out news of their find and was somewhat taken aback when the officer curtly informed him that it was against procedure for him to leave his post. He was so angered by the officer's officious attitude that he later made an official complaint to Commercial Street Police Station, only to be told that the officer had been correct to follow procedure and not leave his post! John Davis, meanwhile, had headed to Commercial Street Police Station, burst through its doors, and breathlessly demanded to see a senior officer.

Moments later Inspector Joseph Chandler was hurrying along Commercial Street. Turning into Hanbury Street, he forced his way through the spectators who were already gathering in the passage of number 29. He ordered that the vicinity be cleared of all sightseers and then sent a constable back to Commercial Street Police Station, instructing him to bring as many reinforcements as possible in order that the crowds might be contained. Another officer was dispatched to fetch Dr. George Bagster Phillips, the divisional police surgeon. Chandler then acquired some sacking from one of the neighbours and used it to cover the body until he arrived.

By the time Phillips arrived at around 6:30 am the crowd outside the house was some several hundred strong. Casting a cursory glance down at the body it was more than obvious to him that the woman was beyond medical help. His testimony at the inquest recalled what he saw:

The left arm was placed across the left breast. The legs were drawn up, the feet resting on the ground, and the knees turned outwards. The face was swollen and turned on the right side. The tongue protruded between the front teeth, but not beyond the lips. The tongue was evidently much swollen. The front teeth were perfect as far as the first molar, top and bottom and very fine teeth they were. The body was terribly mutilated...the stiffness of the limbs was not marked, but was evidently commencing... The throat was dissevered deeply; that the incisions through the skin were jagged and reached right round the neck... On the wooden paling between the yard in question and the next, smears of blood, corresponding to where the head of the deceased lay, were to be seen. These were about 14 inches from the ground, and immediately above the part where the blood from the neck lay.

Later that day the post mortem would reveal that the killer had deftly cut out Annie Chapman's womb and had gone off with it. But at that hour of the morning there was little more that Dr. Phillips could do at the scene so, having pronounced the woman dead, he ordered that she be removed to the Whitechapel Workhouse Infirmary in Eagle Street, off Old Montague Street.

Watched by the agitated crowd, a battered coffin was carried from the building and placed on the police ambulance, which set off eastwards along Hanbury Street, turning right onto Brick Lane. A little before 7 am it pulled up outside

LEFT: It was here on the ground between the steps and the fence that the mutilated body of Annie Chapman was discovered.

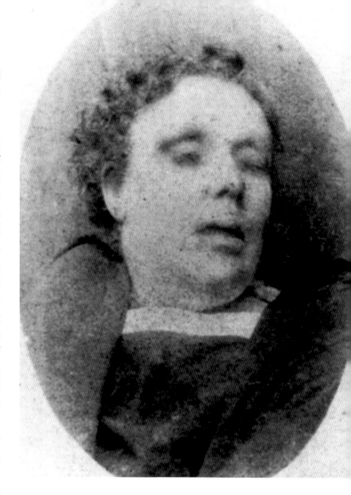

ABOVE: The fact that Annie Chapman's killer had removed and gone off with her womb gave rise to the theory that a medical man might be responsible for the killings.

the mortuary gates where Robert Mann, whose unauthorized stripping and washing down of the body of Mary Nichols was, no doubt, still fresh in the minds of the police, was waiting to receive it. When Inspector Chandler turned up a few minutes later he took one look at Mann and made it clear that nobody was to touch the corpse until Dr. Phillips had completed his postmortem examination. Satisfied that his instructions had been understood, Chandler placed PC Barnes in charge, and headed back to Commercial Street Police Station. Later, both he and Dr. Phillips were furious to discover that within two hours of his departure two nurses, acting on instructions from the clerk of the workhouse guardians, had again stripped and washed the body before a postmortem could be carried out.

Meanwhile a search of the yard of 29 Hanbury Street was under way. It had been evident that the woman's brass rings had been wrenched from a finger, and believing that the killer may have mistaken them for gold, the police made enquiries at pawnbrokers and jewellers' shops; but to no avail. Several of the woman's possessions, namely a small piece of coarse muslin and a comb in a paper case, had been taken from the torn pocket round her waist and laid out at her feet in a way that had suggested to Dr. Phillips that the killer had taken the trouble to 'arrange' them. This has since led to an erroneous yet oft quoted piece of misinformation – that her killer carefully laid Annie Chapman's coins and rings around her feet in a neat crescent, suggesting that the murder was some form of ritualistic or even satanic killing.

Two pills, possibly prescribed during Annie's period in the infirmary, were also discovered, along with part of a torn envelope bearing the crest of the Sussex Regiment. On it was a handwritten 'M' and a postmark reading, 'London, 28 Aug 1888'. Sensing a potential clue to the killer's identity and occupation, Inspector Chandler instigated extensive enquiries to find both the sender and recipient of the letter. Only when they interviewed a lodger at Crossingham's Lodging House, William Stevens, did the police learn that the envelope had been lying on the lodging house mantelpiece for several days. According to Stevens he had watched Annie pick up the envelope in the early hours of the morning of her murder, transfer some pills into it, and leave the room. Stevens' statement ruled out the possibility that the killer had dropped the envelope during the attack, and meant that a promising line of enquiry was abandoned.

Another find, however, was to have far more sinister repercussions. In the corner of the yard, close to the body, there lay a freshly washed leather apron. It later transpired that it belonged to John

LEFT: This old house at the junction of Wilkes Street and Hanbury Street still has the ambience of a bygone era.

Richardson and had been washed and left to dry by his mother, Amelia, a few days earlier. But when some newspapers learnt of its discovery, they were quick to link it to the earlier scare stories concerning the suspect known as Leather Apron, and the anti-Semitism that had been smouldering in the area for the past week suddenly erupted into anti-Jewish unrest that saw Gentile mobs attacking innocent Jews on the streets of the East End. *The East London Advertiser* reported:

A RIOT AGAINST THE JEWS
On Saturday in several quarters of East London the crowds who had assembled in the streets began to assume a very threatening attitude towards the Hebrew population of the district. It was repeatedly asserted that no Englishman could have perpetrated such a horrible crime as that of Hanbury-street, and that it must have been done by a Jew – and forthwith the crowds proceeded to threaten and abuse such of the unfortunate Hebrews as they found in the streets.

Happily, the presence of the large number of police in the streets prevented a riot actually taking place. 'If the panic-stricken people who cry 'Down with the Jews' because they imagine that a Jew has committed the horrible and revolting crimes which have made Whitechapel a place to be dreaded knew anything at all of the Jewish horror of blood itself', writes a correspondent, 'they would pause before they invoked destruction on the head of a peaceful and law-abiding people... That the beast that has made East London a terror is not a Jew I feel assured. There is something too horrible, too unnatural, too un-Jewish, I would say, in the terrible series of murders for an Israelite to be the murderer. There never was a Jew yet who could have steeped himself in such loathsome horrors as those to which publicity has been given. His nature revolts at blood-guiltiness, and the whole theory and practical working of the Whitechapel butchery are opposed to Jewish character.'

Notwithstanding the *East London Advertiser*'s observations about the law-abiding Jewish immigrants, the mob was in need of scapegoats. Egged on by the lurid anti-Semitism of other newspapers, widespread intimidation of innocent Jews gathered pace, and the police were faced with the alarming possibility that a full-scale pogrom was about to occur in the East End of London. In an attempt to forestall it, hundreds of uniformed officers were drafted into the area from other parts of the metropolis, and the mob's agitation was, to an extent, contained.

Throughout September 8th, crowds continued to flock to Hanbury Street, desperate to learn as much as they could about the latest atrocity and get as close as they could to the murder scene. A woman living next door was assuring anyone who would listen that the killer had scrawled on the door of number 29 the alarming message, 'This is the fourth, I will murder sixteen more and then give myself up'. The mob were ready to turn their fear and frustration on any unfortunate man they thought might be responsible, a fact illustrated by a special edition of the *Star* published later that day, which reported how:

Two men were arrested for trifling offences this morning, and on each occasion a maddened crowd ran after the police shouting, 'The murderer's caught!' Another man, injured in a quarrel and carried to the police-station on a stretcher, received similar attention, the crowd fairly mobbing the station and declining to disperse.

A man for whom there has been a warrant out for some time was arrested. In an instant the news spread like wild-fire. From every street, from every court, from the market stands, from the public-houses, rushed forth men and women, all trying to get at the unfortunate captive, declaring he was 'one of the gang', and they meant to lynch him. Thousands gathered, and the police and a private detective had all their work to prevent the man being torn to pieces. The police barrack doors were closed the moment their prisoner had been brought in, and a number of constables did duty outside to prevent the mad onrush of the furious crowd. The inspector in charge informed our reporter the man was arrested for an assault on the police. The crowd sighed at hearing the news, but were not persuaded that the person in question had not something to do with the murder.

Meanwhile the residents of the houses adjoining number 29 had discovered a surprising advantage to their newfound notoriety, and were doing a roaring trade charging an admission fee of one penny to people anxious to view the spot where the body was found. As the *Star* sniffed, 'Several hundreds of people have availed themselves of this opportunity, though all that can be seen are a couple of packing cases from beneath which is the stain of a blood track'.

But on the whole, the people of London were genuinely shocked by the horror of what had happened. Newspapers struggled to convey the sheer brutality of the crime. 'One may search the ghastliest efforts of fiction,' *The Times* told its readers, 'and fail to find anything to surpass these crimes in diabolical audacity…'

RIGHT: A policeman tries to restore order as an agitated mob surrounds Commercial Street Police Station, which can be seen in the background.

CHAPTER EIGHT

SUSPECTS, VIGILANCE AND A STARTLING THEORY

London lies to-day under the spell of a great terror. A nameless reprobate - half beast, half man - is at large, who is daily gratifying his murderous instincts on the most miserable and defenceless classes of the community. There can be no shadow of a doubt now that our original theory was correct, and that the Whitechapel murderer, who has now four, if not five, victims to his knife, is one man, and that man a murderous maniac... Hideous malice, deadly cunning, insatiable thirst for blood - all these are the marks of the mad homicide. The ghoul-like creature who stalks through the streets of London, stalking down his victim... is simply drunk with blood, and he will have more.
Star, September 8th, 1888

At 7 am on September 8th, Mrs Fiddymont, wife of the proprietor of the Prince Albert pub (better known locally as the 'Clean House'), which stood at the corner of Brushfield Street and Steward Street, was standing at the bar talking with a friend of hers named Mary Chappell. Suddenly a man came in whose rough appearance and evil-looking eyes so terrified Mrs Fiddymount that she asked Mary Chappell not to leave her alone with him. He had on a brown stiff hat, pulled down over his eyes and thus partly concealing his face, a dark coat, and no waistcoat. Turning to draw him a glass of ale, Mrs Fiddymont surveyed her customer in the mirror at the back of the bar and noticed that his shirt was badly torn. But what struck her most was a narrow streak of blood under his right ear, parallel with the edge of his shirt. There was also dried blood between the fingers of his hand. When Mary Chappell glanced over at him from the other compartment, he turned his back quickly, thus ensuring that the partition was between them. Downing his drink in one gulp, the man hurried out into the street and headed towards Bishopsgate, closely followed by Mary Chappell. She alerted a passing builder named Joseph Taylor, who hastened after the stranger and came alongside him, being immediately struck by the fact that 'his eyes were as wild as a hawk's'. The man was rather thin, about 5 feet 8 inches tall, aged around 40–50 years, with a ginger-colored moustache, and short sandy hair. He had a shabby genteel look, wore badly fitting pepper-and-salt trousers, and a dark coat. His manner was both nervous and frightened and he walked holding his coat together at the top. Taylor ceased to follow the man, but watched him as far as Dirty Dick's, in Halfmoon Street, where he lost sight of him.

The proximity of the Prince Albert to Hanbury Street meant that the police took the sighting very seriously. Detectives interviewed Mrs Fiddymount and her fellow witnesses, and Abberline himself would later try to forge a link between this bloodstained 'foreigner' and two later suspects.

But for the time being, the police had very little to go on, and, as they threshed around for clues and

OPPOSITE: Brushfield Street and Commercial Street showing just how busy the area around Spitalfields Market was in the 19th century.

ABOVE: Several of the assorted maniacs whom the police arrested as they searched for Jack the Ripper were sent here to Colney Hatch Asylum.

information, press criticism of them intensified. The *Star* advised the local citizens that they had little choice but to take their own measures to defend themselves:

> Now there is only one thing to be done at this moment... the people of the East-end must become their own police. They must form themselves at once into Vigilance Committees... These again should at once devote themselves to volunteer patrol work at night, as well as to general detective service. The unfortunates who are the objects of the man-monster's malignity should be shadowed by one or two of the amateur patrols...

The crowds that thronged around Hanbury Street were ready to take out their frustrations on anyone they thought might be responsible. Press reports about the man seen by Mrs Fiddymont, and of the skullcapped man who was thought to have lured Annie Chapman from the Ten Bells pub at 5 am, continued to fuel the anti-Semitism. Meanwhile, more level-headed journalists began to see the danger of the press campaign, while even others began to doubt the existence of Leather Apron. The *Daily News* commented on the following Monday:

> The public are looking for a monster, and in the legend of 'Leather Apron' the Whitechapel part of them seem to be inventing a monster to look for. This kind of invention ought tobe discouraged in every possible way, or there may soon be murders from panic to add to murders from lust of blood. A touch would fire the whole district in the mood in which it is now.

Once night fell, however, the bravado and anger of the daylight hours were replaced by outright terror. People hurried indoors, afraid to venture out onto the streets. Some of the prostitutes decided that Whitechapel was just too dangerous and moved to other areas. Those that remained retreated to the relative safety of the common lodging houses, abandoning the streets to the patrolling police officers whose plodding, regimented footfall was the only sound to break the silence of the early hours.

Abberline and his colleagues were, by this stage of the investigation, convinced that they were hunting a lone assassin, and a realization of the sheer ruthlessness and cunning of their quarry was beginning to dawn on them. Yet their investigation was hampered by the nature of the crimes and by the fact that his victims were all prostitutes. The killer struck in the dead of night in out-of-the-way places. He left no clues behind him, nor did he have an accomplice who might inform upon him. He was somehow able to prevent his victims from crying out and thus drawing attention to their plight. As far as could be ascertained, there was no motive for the crimes save for the grim satisfaction of mutilating the bodies. And the fact that his victims were all prostitutes meant that they would take him to the places where they knew that they were safe from interruption. As one police officer put it, 'It's not as if he has to wait for his chance, they make that chance for him'.

On September 10th, Sergeant William Thicke went round to 22 Mulberry Street and arrested John Pizer. The police were almost certainly convinced that Pizer was the man known as Leather Apron, so as Sergeant Thicke escorted him into Leman Street Police Station, the feeling that the Whitechapel murderer had been caught must have been running high. An identification parade was held and Pizer was shown first to Mrs Fiddymont, who did not recognize him, and secondly to Emmanuel Violenia, a vagrant, who instantly identified him as a man he'd seen quarreling with a woman outside 29 Hanbury Street in the early hours of the morning of Annie Chapman's murder. He claimed that he had distinctly heard the man threaten to kill the woman by sticking a knife into her. He also claimed that he knew Pizer as Leather Apron. Violenia was then taken to the mortuary where he failed to identify the body of Annie Chapman. Police cross-examination then so discredited his testimony that they quickly dropped him as a witness.

In the meantime, Pizer had provided cast-iron alibis for the nights of the two most recent murders, and by the Tuesday night the police had decided that there was no case against him. He was released without charge. Later, he would appear at Annie Chapman's inquest where, with Sergeant Thicke sitting next to him, he was given the opportunity to publicly clear his name.

On the Monday morning, Inspector Abberline headed to Gravesend where the local police had arrested a 53-year-old ship's cook named William Henry Piggott the night before. He had been making a nuisance of himself in the Pope's Head tavern and had been vociferously declaring his hatred of women. Following his arrest, the police had recovered a paper package that he had left at a local fish shop and found that it contained several items of clothing, amongst them a torn and bloodstained shirt. One of his hands was also injured. Piggott insisted that he had seen a woman fall down in a fit in Whitechapel on Saturday at 4:30 am, and that when he had tried to help her up she bit his hand. Losing his temper he struck her, but then spotted two policemen approaching and ran away. Evidently believing that this might be the man seen by Mrs Fiddymont in the Prince Albert, Abberline brought Piggott back to London for questioning. That afternoon he was placed in a line up, and Mrs Fiddymont and the other two witnesses were brought in to see if they could identify him. Mrs Fiddymont and Joseph Taylor both failed to do so. Mary Chapell picked him out, but would not positively swear that he was the man she had seen. The police, therefore, sent Piggott to the Whitechapel Union Infirmary pending further inquiries, and by September 14th *The Times* was reporting that, 'The police have satisfied themselves that the man Pigott could have had nothing to do with the murders. His movements have been fully accounted for, and he is no longer under surveillance.'

Piggott and Pizer were just two of several suspects that the police hauled in for questioning in the aftermath of Annie Chapman's murder. Indeed, newspaper reports speak of seven men being held at various London police stations at noon on Monday September 10th. The police might not have caught the Whitechapel murderer, but their trawl through the district in search of suspects had certainly yielded a varied batch of lunatics and misfits who were probably better off the streets than on them.

A case at Worship Street Police Court on September 20th demonstrated how the Leather Apron scare was impacting on the lives of the innocent in unforeseen ways. Thomas Mills, aged 59, whose trade was given as cabinetmaker and who had been before the court many times for drunkenness, was brought up again to answer the usual charge. The police constable who had arrested him told the court how he had found the prisoner surrounded by an angry mob that was pulling him about and threatening him with the cry, 'We'll lynch him, he's "Leather Apron".'

For his own safety, Mills was taken into police custody.

In court the prisoner told the magistrate that he had been drunk, but blamed it on the predicament he had found himself in since the start of the Leather Apron scare. 'It's quite true, sir, but what am I to do? Whenever I go out they say I'm 'Leather Apron,' because the papers had published a portrait of the man, and I'm like it. I was out looking for work, and wherever I go they say, 'That's him,' and I can't get work, and I get a drop to drink, and then I get angry.'

Mr Saunders, the magistrate, was not in the least bit sympathetic and told Mills that he had no doubt it was his own fault for getting drunk. If he kept sober, people would not take any notice of his likeness to a picture.

On September 10th a group of local businessmen and tradesmen, many of them Jewish, acted on the *Star*'s call for local action and formed what would become the most famous of the vigilance committees, the Mile End Vigilance Committee. They elected local builder Mr George Akin Lusk as their president. Their stated intention was to aid the police as much as possible, and in their early days they devoted their energies to raising sufficient funds to offer a reward for information. When a public appeal failed to

bring in sufficient money, the committee wrote to the Home Secretary, Henry Matthews, asking that the government either offer a reward, or provide a good reason for not doing so.

The subject of an official reward, or to be more precise the government's refusal to offer one, would remain a bone of contention throughout the entire case. The official line was that rewards did more harm than good in that they encouraged people to come forward and give false information. But this refusal was now starting to rankle in the district; the foreman of the jurors at Mary Nichol's inquest even suggested that the murders of both Chapman and Nichols could have been prevented had the government offered a reward in the wake of Martha Tabram's murder. In fairness to the Home

LEFT: 'The Sensational Interviewer dogs the Detective's footsteps, and throws the strong light of publicity on his work'. As this cartoon from an October 1888 edition of *Punch* shows, there was concern in some quarters that press coverage of the police's methods helped criminals avoid capture.

Office, it is worth noting that several private rewards were offered and that, after Catherine Eddowes' murder, the City of London authorities offered a reward of £500, though none of these resulted in any useful information.

As the arguments for and against a reward were bandied back and forth, some commentators were beginning to view the killer as an inevitable outgrowth of the dreadful social conditions in the area; in an effort to comprehend the incomprehensible, an image was forming in middle class minds of a creature spawned by the vice and squalour of the slums. On September 18th, in a letter to *The Times*, Sidney Godolphin Osborne warned:

> However abhorrent in all cruel, filthy detail are the murders to which public attention is now so painfully called, however hard it may be to believe that they could occur in any civilized community, the fact remains that they have been so committed. Whatever the theories to account for them, whether or not the perpetrators may be yet discovered, they have been the means of affording to us a warning it will be at our extreme peril to neglect. We have far too long been content to know that within a walk of palaces and mansions, where all that money can obtain secures whatever can contribute to make human life one of luxury... there have existed tens of thousands of our fellow creatures begotten and reared in an atmosphere of godless brutality, a species of human sewage, the very drainage of the vilest production of ordinary vice, such sewage ever on the increase, and in its increase for ever developing fresh depths of degradation...
>
> We may choose to ignore the fact, but there is not a shadow of doubt in the minds of those who have made this deprived race a study, that of both sexes it may be said they scarce have passed childhood before they fall into the grosser sins of that adult life which is their daily street examples.
>
> Just so long as the dwellings of this race continue in their present condition, their whole surroundings a sort of warren of foul alleys garnished with the flaring lamps of the gin shops, and offering to all sorts of lodgers, for all conceivable wicked purposes, every possible accommodation to further brutalize, we shall have still to go on - affecting astonishment that in such a state of things we have outbreaks from time to time of the horrors of the present day.

Osborne's letter (signed simply SGO) inspired one of the most readily recognizable images associated with the Ripper crimes, *Punch's* cartoon 'The Nemesis of Neglect'. It showed a shrouded, hollow-eyed phantom holding aloft a fearsome-looking knife, drifting through the miasmic slums of the East End. The cartoon's caption reiterated the image:

> There floats a phantom on the slum's foul air,
> Shaping, to eyes which have the gift of seeing,
> Into the Spectre of that loathly lair.
> Face it - for vain is fleeing!
> Red-handed, ruthless, furtive, unerect,
> 'Tis murderous Crime - the Nemesis of Neglect!

Social reformers had begun to realize that the murders could be effectively utilized to spear-head change in the neighbourhood. The *Lancet* pointed out that 'modern society is more promptly awakened to a sense of duty by the knife of a murderer than by the pens of many earnest writers...'

The *Daily Telegraph* lectured its readers:

'DARK ANNIE'S' spirit still walks Whitechapel, unavenged by Justice... yet even this forlorn and despised citizeness of London cannot be said to have suffered in vain. On the contrary, she has effected more by her death than many long speeches in Parliament and countless columns of letters to the newspapers could have brought about. She has forced innumerable people who never gave a serious thought before to the subject to realize how it is and where it is that our vast floating population - the waifs and strays of our thoroughfares - live and sleep at nights, and what sort of accommodation our rich and enlightened capital provides for them, after so many Acts of Parliament passed to improve the dwellings of the poor... 'Dark ANNIE'S' dreadful end has compelled a hundred thousand Londoners to reflect what it must be like to have no home at all except the 'common kitchen' of a low lodging-house; to sit there, sick and weak and bruised and wretched, for lack of fourpence with which to pay for the right of a 'doss'; to be turned out after midnight to earn the requisite pence, anywhere and anyhow; and in course of earning it to come across your murderer and to caress your assassin.

On September 19th, Canon Barnett, the vicar of St Jude's Church on Commercial Street, founder of Toynbee Hall and ardent mover for social reform in the area wrote to *The Times*:

Sir, - Whitechapel horrors will not be in vain if 'at last' the public conscience awakes to consider the life which these horrors reveal. The murders were, it may almost be said, bound to come; generation could not follow generation in lawless intercourse, children could not be familiarized with scenes of degradation, community in crime could not be the bond of society and the end of all be peace.

He pointed out that, 'The greater part of Whitechapel is as orderly as any part of London, and the life of most of its inhabitants is more moral than that of many whose vices are hidden by greater wealth'. However, the evil quarter mile onto which his church adjoined, and where the victims of the recent murders had lodged, needed to be dealt with 'strongly and adequately'. The first requirement was an increase of police officer numbers in the neighbourhood. The Home Office, he complained, had 'never authorized the employment of a sufficient force to keep decent order inside the criminal quarters'. Secondly, adequate lighting was essential. 'Without doubt...dark passages lend themselves to evil deeds.' He also inadvertently highlighted a reason why the murderer could escape, possibly bloodstained, into the teeming streets of the neighbourhood without being noticed. Calling for the closure of the area's many slaughterhouses, he pointed out that 'At present animals are daily slaughtered in the midst of

Whitechapel, the butchers with their blood stains are familiar among the street passengers, and sights are common which tend to brutalize ignorant natures.'

On September 24th, George Bernard Shaw wrote to the *Star* and offered his own intriguing theory for the killer's motive:

> SIR, - Will you allow me to make a comment on the success of the Whitechapel murderer in calling attention for a moment to the social question? Private enterprise has succeeded where Socialism failed. Whilst we conventional Social Democrats were wasting our time on education, agitation, and organization, some independent genius has taken the matter in hand, and by simply murdering and disembowelling four women, converted the proprietary press to an inept sort of communism.

No doubt Shaw's tongue was very firmly in his cheek when he suggested that the murderer was a social reformer, but there is little doubt that the Whitechapel murders had succeeded in drawing attention to the dreadful living conditions in the area, and several of the improvements that took place over the next few years can be attributed to this.

As the socially-minded began to focus their attention on the need for change in the area, the police continued to arrest suspects. In the early hours of September 18th, PC John Johnson of the City Police was walking his beat along Minories when he heard a loud cry of 'Murder!' It was coming from a walled-in yard – a notorious trouble spot by the name of Three Kings' Court. Hurrying through the alleyway that led into it from Minories, Johnson found a man and a woman standing together there.

When Johnson asked the man what he was doing he received the brusque reply, 'Nothing'.

The woman was evidently terrified and begged him, 'Oh policeman do take me out of this!'

Johnson escorted the couple out of the court and told the man to be on his way. As the man vanished, the woman turned to Johnson and exclaimed, 'Dear me. He frightened me very much when he pulled that big knife out.'

Johnson's jaw no doubt fell open. 'Why didn't you tell me that at the time?' he asked.

'I was too much frightened.'

Johnson conducted a quick search of the area but could find no trace of the man. It must have been a very nervous Johnson who informed his superiors that he might have had the killer and let him go.

As it transpired, the man had headed over to Whitechapel High Street, where he got into a heated and drunken exchange with a coffee stallholder and a youth named Alexander Finlay. Having pulled out a long-bladed knife, the man chased Finlay around the coffee stall and attempted to stab him, whereupon a constable arrived and took the man into police custody. The man was a German hairdresser named Charles Ludwig and the police evidently thought him a good murder suspect. When he appeared at Thames Magistrates' Court, charged with being drunk and disorderly and with threatening to stab Finlay, the magistrate called him a dangerous character and remanded him in custody for a week. As Ludwig languished in prison, the police conducted rigorous investigations into his background and character. When he next appeared in court, on September 25th, Abberline asked that he be remanded again and the magistrate complied. But his innocence was proved conclusively when, in the early hours of September 30th, with Ludwig safely in custody, the Whitechapel murderer struck gain, thus absolving him of any involvement.

On September 19th, Sir Charles Warren wrote to the Home Office to update them on progress, or to be more precise, the lack of progress in the police investigation: 'A great number of clues have been examined and exhausted without finding anything suspicious. A large staff of men are employed and every point is being examined which seems to offer any prospect of a discovery.'

He also mentioned three suspects that the police favoured. The first was Jacob Isenschmid, an insane pork butcher from Switzerland who had been arrested at Holloway and was now in an asylum. Abberline had written of him on September 18th, 'Although at present we are unable to procure any evidence to connect him with the murders, he appears to be the most likely person that has come under our notice to have committed the crimes'.

Apparently two doctors, Dr. Cowan and Dr. Landseer, had told the police that this man, whom they knew to be a lunatic, was the murderer. His landlord told the police that he was absent from his lodgings on the night of Annie Chapman's murder. His estranged wife, Mary, told Sergeant Thicke that although her husband was violent she did not think he would 'injure anyone but me. I think he would kill me if he had the chance.' Abberline was struck by the fact that Isenschmid bore a strong resemblance to the man seen by Mrs Fiddymont in the Prince Albert, and the fact that her name disappears from police records after this suggests that she may have identified him as such. But, as with Ludwig, Isenschmid was to be absolved: for, on September 30th, when the killer struck again, the mad Swiss pork butcher was caged in an asylum.

Warren's second suspect was Oswald Puckeridge who had been 'released from an asylum on August 4th [and who] has threatened to rip people up. He is being looked for but cannot be found as yet'. Not a great deal has been found about Puckeridge, and even less is known as to why the police suspected him. It would seem that they may have traced him and eliminated him as a suspect, since he was not included in later police reports and correspondence.

The final suspect is even more elusive, since Warren doesn't identify him but merely states that, 'A brothel keeper who will not give her address or name writes to say that a man living in her house was seen with blood on him on morning of murder. She described his appearance and said where he might be seen. When the detectives came near him he bolted, got away and there is no clue to the writer of the letter.'

Meanwhile, Dr. George Bagster Phillips, the divisional police surgeon who had examined Annie's body as it lay in the back yard of 29 Hanbury Street, suggested at her inquest that the reason for her murder may well have been to secure her womb, given that her killer had removed it and taken it away. Furthermore, the speed and skill with which he did it suggested that he might well have possessed some anatomical knowledge.

The police themselves were rapidly coming around to the view that the murderer was probably a lunatic and that he possibly possessed surgical knowledge. As a result, three medical students who had recently spent time in asylums were traced and interviewed. But as with so many avenues of enquiry, this led to a dead end; one by one, the students were exonerated of any involvement.

Suspect after suspect was evidently being brought in throughout September, often on very tenuous grounds, and as the end of the month approached it was becoming obvious that the police were no nearer catching the killer than they had been at the beginning of the month. On September 22nd, *Punch* summed up their efforts with a cartoon entitled 'Blind-Man's Buff'. It showed a blindfolded policeman being spun around by a rough-looking group of villains. The accompanying caption read 'TURN ROUND THREE TIMES, AND CATCH WHOM YOU MAY!' In the same issue it treated its readers to 'A Detective's Diary':

Monday. - Papers full of the latest tragedy. One of them suggested that the assassin was a man who wore a blue coat. Arrested three blue-coat wearers on suspicion.

Tuesday. - The blue coats proved innocent. Released. Evening journal threw out a hint that the deed might have been perpetrated by a soldier. Found a small drummer-boy drunk and incapable. Conveyed him to the Station-house.

Wednesday. - Drummer-boy released. Letter of anonymous correspondent to daily journal declaring that the outrage could only have been committed by a sailor. Decoyed petty officer of Penny Steamboat on shore, and suddenly arrested him.

Thursday. - Petty officer allowed to go. Hint thrown out in the correspondence columns that the crime might be traceable to a lunatic. Noticed an old gentleman purchasing a copy of *Maiwa's Revenge*. Seized him.

Friday. - Lunatic dispatched to an asylum. Anonymous letter received, denouncing local clergyman as the criminal. Took the reverend gentleman into custody.

Saturday. - Eminent ecclesiastic set at liberty with an apology. Ascertain in a periodical that it is thought just possible that the Police may have committed the crime themselves. At the call of duty, finished week by arresting myself!

On September 26th, at Annie Chapman's inquest, Coroner Baxter began his summing up. Dr. Phillips' comments about the murderer's motive and possible anatomical knowledge had paved the way for Coroner Baxter to astound all present with his own sensational theory:

The body has not been dissected, but the injuries have been made by some one who had considerable anatomical skill and knowledge. There are no meaningless cuts. It was done by one who knew where to find what he wanted, what difficulties he would have to contend against, and how he should use his knife, so as to abstract the organ without injury to it. No unskilled person could have known where to find it, or have recognized it when it was found. For instance, no mere slaughterer of animals could have carried out these operations. It must have been some one accustomed to the post-mortem room. The conclusion that the desire was to possess the missing part seems overwhelming.

Here was a bogeyman to out-bogey Leather Apron – a doctor, or at least a person with some amount of medical knowledge, wandering the streets of Whitechapel in search of wombs, presumably for research purposes. The revelation was met with a murmur of disdainful disapproval. But Baxter wasn't finished:

It has been suggested that the criminal is a lunatic with morbid feelings. This may or may not be the case; but the object of the murderer appears palpably shown by the facts, and it is not necessary to assume lunacy, for it is clear that there is a market for the object of the murder. To show you this, I must mention a fact which at the same time proves the assistance which publicity and the newspaper press afford in the detection of crime. Within a few hours of the issue of the morning papers containing a report of the medical evidence given at the last sitting of the Court, I received a communication from an officer of one of our great medical schools, that they had information which might or might not have a distinct bearing on our inquiry. I attended at the first opportunity, and was told by the sub-curator of the Pathological Museum that some months ago an American had called on him, and asked him to procure a number of specimens of the organ that was missing in the deceased. He stated his willingness to give £20 for each, and explained that his object was to issue an actual specimen with each copy of a publication on which he was then engaged. Although he was told that his wish was impossible to be complied with, he still urged his request. He desired them preserved, not in spirits of wine, the usual medium, but in glycerine, in order to preserve them in a flaccid condition, and he wished them sent to America direct. It is known that this request was repeated to another institution of a similar character. Now, is it not possible that the knowledge of this demand may have incited some abandoned wretch to possess himself of a specimen... His object is clearly divulged. His anatomical skill carries him out of the category of a common criminal, for his knowledge could only have been obtained by assisting at post-mortems, or by frequenting the post-mortem room.

It is important to remember that Baxter did not state that the doctor in question was the murderer, but merely gave it as his opinion that the offer may have inspired someone to commit the murder for financial gain. The press, though, were quick to dub his revelation 'The Burke and Hare Theory' and praised him for having the courage to make it public. Naturally the medical profession was quick to refute it. On September 29th the *Lancet* lamented that:

The public mind - ever too ready to cast mud at legitimate research - will hardly fail to be excited to a pitch of animosity against anatomists and curators, which may take a long while to subside. And, what is equally deplorable, the revelation thus made by the coroner, which so dramatically startled the public last Wednesday evening, may probably lead to a diversion from the real track of the murderer, and thus defeat rather than serve the ends of justice. We believe the story to be highly improbable...

The *British Medical Journal* went further and scotched the theory once and for all:

It is true that enquiries were made at one or two medical schools early last year by a foreign physician, who was spending some time in London, as to the possibility of securing certain parts of the body for purposes of scientific investigation. No large sum, however, was offered. The person in question was a physician of the highest reputability... and he left London fully eighteen months ago. There was never any real foundation for the hypothesis, and the information communicated, which was not at all of the nature the public has been led to believe, was due to the erroneous interpretation by a minor official of a question which he had overheard and to which a negative reply was given. This theory may be dismissed, and is, we believe, no longer entertained even by its author.

It is significant that Coroner Baxter did not revive his theory at the inquest into the death of the next victim, Elizabeth Stride. But the image of Dr. Jack the Ripper had taken shape in the minds of the public at large, and it remains one of the most popular images of the murderer to this day.

On the streets of Whitechapel, the fact that there had been no new murders since September 8th meant that the fear and panic were beginning to subside. Many of the prostitutes had returned to their old haunts. In the pubs people chatted in animated tones about the revelations that had emerged from the inquests, particularly Coroner Baxter's sensational claims.

On September 22nd a woman was murdered at Birtley Fell, near Gateshead, in the north of England and inevitably comparisons were made with the Whitechapel murders.

As the end of September approached, a journalist from the *Daily News* took an evening stroll through the area. In Hanbury Street, he met with a respectable looking elderly man and observed, 'There seems to be little apprehension of further mischief by this assassin at large.'

'No, very little', was the cheerful reply. 'People, most of 'em, think he's gone to Gateshead.'

Three days later, the Whitechapel murderer would murder twice in less than an hour.

CHAPTER NINE

'LONG LIZ' STRIDE

Elizabeth or 'Long Liz' Stride spent the last afternoon of her life cleaning rooms in the lodging house at 32 Flower and Dean Street, where she had lived on and off for the previous six years. The deputy keeper, Elizabeth Tanner, paid her six pence for the chores and by 6:30 pm Elizabeth was slaking her thirst in the nearby Queen's Head pub at the junction of Fashion and Commercial Streets. By 7 pm she had returned to the lodging house, and was, according to fellow resident Charles Preston – from whom she borrowed a clothes brush – dressed 'ready to go out'. Having chatted briefly with another lodger, Catherine Lane, Liz Stride left the lodging house at around 7:30 pm.

It rained heavily that night and at 11 pm J. Best and John Gardner saw her sheltering in the doorway of the Bricklayer's Arms on Settles Street. She was in the company of a man who was about 5 feet 5 inches tall. He had a black moustache, sandy eyelashes, and was wearing a black morning suit together with a billycock hat.

According to Best, 'They did not appear willing to go out. He was hugging and kissing her, and as he seemed a respectably dressed man, we were rather astonished at the way he was going on with the woman.'

The two men couldn't resist a little lighthearted banter at the couple's expense and remarked to the woman, 'Watch out, that's Leather Apron getting round you!'

Embarrassed by the chaffing, the couple 'went off like a shot'. Best and Gardner watched them hurry off through the rain towards Commercial Road.

At some stage in the next 45 minutes, Elizabeth Stride made her way to nearby Berner Street, a relatively short thoroughfare that was lined with two-floor houses. A little way along on the right-hand side were the gates into Dutfield's Yard, a narrow court which was lined on its right side by the wall of the International Working Men's Educational Club, founded in 1884 by a group of Jewish Socialists, and on its left side by the wall of 42 Berner Street, behind which was a row of cottages. At the top of the yard there stood a work premises and a disused stable. On this particular Saturday about a hundred people had crammed into the club to debate the topic 'Why Jews should be Socialists'. The meeting broke up at around 11:30 pm and the majority of the members headed home. About a dozen people, however, stayed on and gathered in the upstairs room where they either chatted or started singing. Louis Diemshutz, the club steward, had gone out to hawk jewellry at Crystal Palace, but his wife who lived with him on the premises was overseeing proceedings.

At around 11:45 pm, William Marshall, a laborer who lived at 64 Berner Street, was standing outside his lodgings when he noticed a man and woman outside number 63. They both seemed quite sober, and as he watched them they began to kiss. Marshall heard the man remark to the woman, 'You would say anything but your prayers'. The couple then moved off, heading in the direction of Dutfield's Yard. Marshall described the man as middle-aged and stout, with the appearance of a clerk. He was around

OPPOSITE: Dutfield's Yard, where Elizabeth Stride was murdered, is visible in this photograph as the gate with the carriage wheel above it.

Going to her doom

5 feet 6 inches tall, clean-shaven, and respectably dressed. He wore a small black cut-away coat, dark trousers, and a round cap with a small sailor-like peak.

At 12:30 am, PC William Smith proceeded along Berner Street on his beat and noticed a man and a woman on the opposite side of the road to Dutfield's Yard. The man was approximately 28 years old, with a dark complexion and a small dark moustache. He was about 5 feet 7 inches tall, had on a dark overcoat, a hard felt deerstalker, and dark clothing. The woman, whom Smith later identified as Elizabeth Stride, had a flower pinned to her jacket. However, the couple did nothing to arouse Smith's suspicion, so he continued on his beat to Commercial Road.

Morris Eagle, who had chaired the earlier debate at the International Working Men's Educational Club, left the premises at around 12:15 am to walk his 'young lady' home. Returning to the club at 12:35 am he found the front door locked, so went through the gates into Dutfield's Yard, and entered the club via its back door. He saw nothing on the ground by the gates, and was sure he would have noticed if a man and woman had been in the yard. However, since the yard itself was pitch black, he was not able to say for certain if the body of Elizabeth Stride was there at that time.

The most important witness to have seen Elizabeth Stride in the half hour before her body was discovered in Dutfield's Yard was a Hungarian Jew by the name of Israel Schwartz. He turned into Berner Street at around 12:45 am and noticed a man walking ahead of him. The man stopped to talk to a woman who was standing in the gateway of Dutfield's Yard. Later, Schwartz was emphatic that the woman he had seen was Elizabeth Stride. Since it is likely that Israel Schwartz witnessed the early stages of Elizabeth Stride's murder (and is therefore possibly the only person ever to have seen one of Jack the Ripper's victims actually being murdered), his statement is worth close scrutiny, even though he spoke no English and had to give his evidence through an interpreter. The police seem to have taken him very seriously as a witness, and there is a high probability that the man seen by Schwartz was the murderer.

According to Schwartz, the man was about 5 feet 5 inches tall, aged around 30, with dark hair, a fair complexion, and a small brown moustache. He had a full face, broad shoulders, and appeared to be slightly intoxicated. As Schwartz watched, the man tried to pull the woman into the street, but then spun her around and threw her onto the footway, whereupon the woman screamed three times, but not very loudly. Israel Schwartz apparently believed that he was witnessing a domestic attack, so crossed the road to avoid getting involved. As he did so, he saw a second man standing, lighting his pipe. As Schwartz passed him, the man who was attacking the woman called out the word 'Lipski' (see page 17), apparently to this second man, at which point the second man began to follow him. Schwartz panicked and began to run and had managed to lose his pursuer by the time he reached the nearby railway arch. This man, Schwartz said, was aged about 35, was around 5 feet 11 inches tall, had a fresh complexion, light brown hair, a brown moustache, and wore a dark overcoat with an old black hard felt hat.

The presence of the second man at the scene is something of a mystery. It has suggested to some that the killer had an accomplice. However, the police seem to have traced him and eliminated him as a suspect. In a report dated October 19th, 1888, Chief Inspector Swanson wrote that 'the police apparently do not suspect the second man', although we do not know why this should have been.

At 1 am Louis Diemshutz, the steward of the International Working Men's Educational Club, returned to Dutfield's Yard from Westow Hill Market, near Crystal Palace, where he had spent the day hawking cheap jewellery. As he turned his pony and cart into the yard, his pony shied to the left and refused to go any further. Looking into the yard, Diemshutz saw a dark shape lying on the ground close to the wall of the club. Leaning forward he prodded it with his whip and tried to lift it. When this proved unsuccessful, he jumped down to investigate and struck a match to get a better view. It was windy that night and the match was extinguished almost immediately, but in the brief seconds of flickering light, he saw that it was a woman lying on the ground. For some reason he thought it might be his wife, and so he went into the club by the side entrance to see if she was there.

Finding his wife safe, he told several club members, 'There's a woman lying in the yard, but I cannot say whether she is drunk or dead'.

Taking a candle, Diemshutz returned to the yard with several other club members. Now he noticed blood by the body and those present saw to their horror that the woman's throat had been cut.

The various club members rushed from the yard and hurried off into the surrounding streets to find a police constable. Deimshutz and a companion headed along Fairclough Street shouting 'Murder' and 'Police'. At its junction with Christian Street, they met Edward Spooner. He asked what all the fuss was about and when they told him, he returned with them to Dutfield's Yard where around 15 people were now gathered. Spooner stooped down, lifted the woman's chin and found it to be slightly warm. As Spooner tilted her head back, Diemschutz got his first glimpse of just how terrible her throat wound was.

'I could see that her throat was fearfully cut,' he told a journalist later that day. 'There was a great gash in it over two inches wide.'

There was a stream of blood running from the woman's throat and up the yard towards the door of the club. There was also a doubled up piece of paper in the woman's right hand, which later turned out to be a packet of cachous, or breath fresheners.

Morris Eagle and another

RIGHT: So dark was Dutfield's Yard that Elizabeth Stride's injuries were only apparent by lamplight.

club member had headed out of Berner Street and gone right along Commercial Road. Here they met PC Henry Lamb and told him, 'Come on! There has been another murder.'

Lamb alerted PC Edward Collins and together they followed the two men back to Dutfield's Yard, where the crowd had now swelled to some 20–30 people. Lamb ordered the bystanders to keep back, lest they get blood on their clothing and 'find themselves in trouble', and told Collins to go at once for Dr. Frederick William Blackwell, who lived at 100 Commercial Road. He then sent Morris Eagle to Leman Street Police Station to summon further assistance. As the two men headed off, Lamb stooped down and felt the woman's face. It was still slightly warm. However, when he felt her wrist he could detect no sign of a pulse.

When asked by the coroner at the subsequent inquest whether the woman's clothing had been disturbed, Lamb replied, 'No. I could scarcely see her boots'. He added, 'She looked like she had been quietly laid down.'

Dr. Blackwell arrived in the yard at 1:16 am and having pronounced the woman dead, gave it as his opinion that she had been dead for between 20–30 minutes. He noted that the woman was wearing a check silk scarf, the bow of which was turned to the left and pulled tightly. At the inquest he stated that he believed the killer had first taken hold of the back of the silk scarf, and pulled his victim backwards onto the ground. However, he could not be certain whether the woman's throat was cut while she was standing or after she had been pulled backwards. Once the killer had cut her throat, slicing through the windpipe, she would not have been able to cry out, and would have bled to death within about a minute and a half.

Shortly after Dr. Blackwell's arrival, PC Lamb gave orders to close the gates into Dutfield's Yard and told everybody to remain where they were. He then carried out a search of the club premises, examining people's hands and clothing for bloodstains in the process. Having found nothing suspicious, he went round to the cottages at the rear of 42 Berner Street and woke the residents, who had apparently remained asleep throughout the excitement of the previous half hour. The residents appeared very frightened, and when they asked Lamb what had happened he told them 'nothing much' to avoid alarming them further.

Lamb then returned to the body to find that Inspector West, Inspector Pinhorn, and Dr. Phillips had arrived at the scene. Inspector Reid was alerted by telegram at 1:25 am and headed directly to Berner Street from Commercial Street Police Station. When he arrived, Phillips and Blackwell were examining the woman's throat. All the

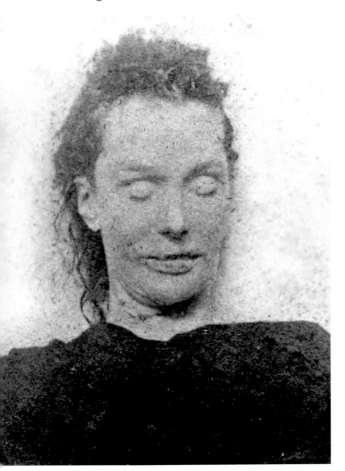

LEFT: The mortuary photograph of Elizabeth Stride.

people in the yard were then interrogated and their names and addresses taken. Once they had given a satisfactory account of themselves and their movements, and their hands and pockets had been inspected and searched, they were allowed to leave. A more thorough search was then made of the cottages and the names of the residents ascertained. Hopes of apprehending the killer in his hiding place were briefly raised when the door of a loft was found to be locked from the inside, but on forcing it open the police found it empty. Reid then minutely inspected the wall in the vicinity of the body and found no traces of blood on it. At 4:30 am, the body was removed to St George's Mortuary in Cable Street and at 5 am PC Albert Collins washed the blood away from the yard.

The fact that Elizabeth Stride only had her throat cut and had not been disemboweled suggested that the killer had been interrupted in the course of the murder. It is possible that he was commencing his mutilations when Diemshutz entered the yard, and that he jumped back into the shadows to avoid being seen. Indeed, it could have been this sudden movement that startled the pony, causing it to shy to the left. Later that day, it dawned on Diemshutz that the killer may have been hiding in the shadows just a few inches away from him as he made his grisly discovery. With Diemshutz distracted, the murderer no doubt slipped out into Berner Street and made good his escape. No weapon had been found; no clues had been discovered. Yet again the Whitechapel murderer had killed within yards or even feet of numerous people, had possibly been interrupted in the process, and yet, as on the other occasions, he had simply melted away unseen into the night. Or had he? On October 1st, the *Star* newspaper carried the following report:

> From two different sources we have the story that a man when passing through Church-lane at about half-past one, saw a man sitting on a door-step and wiping his hands. As every one is on the look out for the murderer the man looked at the stranger with a certain amount of suspicion, whereupon he tried to conceal his face. He is described as a man who wore a short jacket and a sailor's hat.

The man's jacket and sailor's hat are certainly similar to the clothing worn by the men or man seen with Stride by William Marshall and Israel Schwartz. There is also a similarity to the clothing and appearance of the man seen by Joseph Lawende outside Mitre Square (see page 89). Unfortunately the report is uncorroborated, and there is no mention of the sighting in police records, or at least if there was, it has not survived. There is also a problem of timing, since at 1:30 am the murderer was apparently standing outside Mitre Square chatting with Catherine Eddowes. It is possible that the witness, who, like most people in the area, was unlikely to have possessed a watch, was estimating the time that he had passed along Church Lane, and that the sighting actually took place earlier. But if genuine, it does give an idea of the route taken by Elizabeth Stride's killer when he left Berner Street. Aware that Berner Street would soon be the epicenter of the search for him, he would have been anxious to get away as quickly as possible. He was probably quite fortunate that Diemshutz didn't raise the alarm immediately but instead went into the club. This gave him vital minutes in which to escape the yard. With bloodstained hands, an escape along the brightly lit and fairly busy Commercial Road would have been risky, but a left turn out of Dutfield's Yard would have brought him within seconds to a dark, narrow thoroughfare known as Batty's Gardens. From here he could have taken any number of routes, Church Lane being one of them. Whichever route he took, within half an hour he had found his way into the City of London and had met his next victim.

CHAPTER TEN

FALSEHOODS, FALLACIES AND FABRICATIONS

Identifying the Berner Street victim proved more difficult than any of the others. In life, Elizabeth Stride had without doubt been a self-dramatising fantasist; in death she was to prove even more elusive, at least at first. Her identification was hampered by the appearance of a mysterious lady named Mary Malcolm, who spun the police and then the inquest an elaborate yarn that delayed a definite identification by almost three weeks. Mrs Malcolm was the wife of a tailor and lived at 50 Eagle Street, off Red Lion Square, Holborn. She had a sister by the name of Elizabeth who was 37 years old and who had been living in an East End lodging house. Some years ago, this sister had married a respectable Bath wine merchant by the name of Watts, but had then 'brought disgrace on her family' when her husband found her in bed with a porter. He sent her and their two children, a boy and a girl, back to live with her 'poor mother'. The girl died and the boy was sent to a boarding school, his fees being paid by Mr Watts' elderly sister.

Elizabeth Watts had then moved in with a man in Poplar who ran a coffee shop. In 1885 she suffered another setback when this man went to sea and was drowned in a shipwreck. After that, Liz Watts had gone well and truly off the rails. According to her sister Mary, 'Drink was a failing with her [and she had]… been before the Thames Police Court magistrate on charges of drunkenness'. On one occasion Liz had even left a naked baby outside Mrs Malcolm's door, the result of an illicit affair with 'some policeman or another'. The Malcolms had to keep the child until Liz 'fetched it away'. When asked by the coroner what her sister did for a living, Mrs Malcolm assumed a grave demeanour and replied, 'I had my doubts'. However, Mary had gone out of her way to ensure that her sister didn't starve, and on every Saturday at 4 pm for the last two and a half years, Mrs Malcolm had met with her errant sibling at the corner of Chancery Lane and had given her two shillings to pay for her lodgings. But on the Saturday just gone, Liz had failed to appear. Mrs Malcolm had, in fact, last seen her alive on the previous Thursday when Liz turned up at her place of work to ask for 'a little assistance'. Mrs Malcolm had given her a shilling and a little short jacket.

At 1:20 am on Sunday September 30th, Mrs Malcolm was lying in bed when she felt a 'kind of pressure' on her breast. This was followed by three kisses on her cheek, which she also heard, as they were 'quite distinct'. This led her to believe that some tragedy had befallen her sister at that instant, and when later that day she read of the Berner Street murder, she at once suspected the victim to be her sibling. The long-suffering Mary Malcolm quickly headed over to Whitechapelto inform the police. On first seeing the body at the mortuary she was unable to identify it as her sister's (at the inquest, she excused her

OPPOSITE: At around the time of Elizabeth Stride's murder, Leon Goldstein left a coffee shop here in Spectacle Alley and hurried home along Berner Street clutching a black bag. The fact he was mistaken for the murderer furnished the Ripper legend with the black doctor's bag.

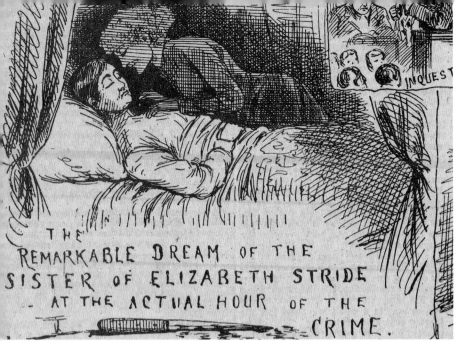

THE REMARKABLE DREAM OF THE SISTER OF ELIZABETH STRIDE
AT THE ACTUAL HOUR OF THE CRIME.

LEFT: As Mary Malcolm lay in bed around the time of Elizabeth Stride's murder, she felt three kisses on her cheek. This convinced her that the murdered woman was her sister, whose spirit had come to say goodbye.

failure on the basis of her only having seen it by gaslight). However she was able to make a positive identification the next day – not, it should be noted, from her sister's facial features, but from a black mark on her leg, which was, she said, the result of Liz's having been bitten by an adder when they were girls. At the inquest Mary Malcolm also revealed that they had another sister and a brother, neither of whom had seen Liz for years. The disgrace of it all, she told the coroner with trembling lip, would kill her other sister. Then, bursting into profuse tears, Mary wailed to an open-jawed courtroom how she had stoically 'kept this shame from everyone'. Poor Mary Malcolm.

And poor Mrs Elizabeth Stokes, wife of Joseph Stokes, a brickmaker of 5 Charles Street, Tottenham, who hobbled into the Coroner's Court on October 23rd to reveal that she was in fact Mary Malcolm's sister, the former Elizabeth Watts of Bath. Her first husband had died, after which she had suffered a mental breakdown, but her character had remained good. There had been no adulterous flings with a porter or a policeman, no cuckolded husband, and no children maintained by an aunt, or, for that matter, left naked on her sister's doorstep. She was now being accused of living bigamously with her second husband, and neighbours' tongues were wagging.

'My sister I have not seen for years', an indignant Elizabeth Stokes told the Coroner's Court. 'She has given me a dreadful character. Her evidence is all false… This has put me to dreadful trouble… It is a shame my sister should say what she has about me, and that the innocent should suffer for the guilty.'

Of Mrs Malcolm, however, there was no sign.

'Is Mrs Malcolm here?' asked the Coroner angrily, no doubt wanting her to provide him with an explanation.

'No, Sir,' was Inspector Edmund Reid's succinct reply.

But what was Mary Malcolm's motivation for the elaborate yarn, and why did she stick to her story while under oath, against hostile questioning from both the coroner and the police, who made it quite plain that they didn't believe a word of her story? It has been suggested that she may have been a macabre ghoul who just wanted to see the body of the murder victim. If this was the case, then why did she not simply walk away on the Sunday or Monday once she had viewed the body at the mortuary? Why perjure herself under oath? Others argue that she was simply an attention seeker, enjoying her time in the spotlight, even if it meant libeling her innocent and blameless sister. This is possible, although journalists reporting her testimony frequently commented that she seemed truly grieved by her loss.

One final explanation is that she genuinely believed that Elizabeth Stride was Elizabeth Watts. Is it possible that Stride, who was capable of an extreme economy with the truth at the best of times, had been impersonating Elizabeth Watts in order to illicit funds from her sister?

We can only guess at Mrs Malcolm's motivation. She is just one of those tantalizing aspects of the case that cropped up, added another element of mystery, and then disappeared without trace. And the murder of Elizabeth Stride was to add two more twists to the tale that would result in several well-known and frequently quoted fallacies that have since become an integral part of the Jack the Ripper legend.

The first came courtesy of Matthew Packer, a greengrocer who lived at and traded from 44 Berner Street, two doors south of the International Working Men's Educational Club. An *Evening News* reporter politely described him as a respectable and hardworking person who was 'a little past the prime of life'. At 9 am on the September 30th, Sergeant Stephen White called on Packer in the course of his door-to-door enquiries. Packer was adamant that both he and his wife had neither seen nor heard anything untoward during the night. Two days later, Packer was visited by Grand and Batchelor, two private detectives employed by the *Evening News* and the Whitechapel Vigilance Committee. He had, it seems, remembered an important detail, which had somehow slipped his mind when White had called a few days before. He told the two private detectives that he had sold grapes to a man and a woman from his shop window at around 11:45 pm on the night of the murder. The man, he said, was aged about 35, was around 5 feet 7 inches tall, and was of stout, square build. He wore a wide-awake hat, dark clothes, and had the general appearance of a clerk, or as Packer put it when expanding on his story to an *Evening News* reporter, 'I am certain that he wasn't what I should call a working man or anything like us folks that live around here'.

Packer recalled how the man had asked him, 'I say, old man, how do you sell your grapes?'

'Six pence a pound the black 'uns, sir, and four pence a pound the white 'uns', was Packer's response.

Turning to the woman, the man asked, 'Which will you have, my dear, black or white? You shall have whichever you like best'.

The woman chose the black ones.

Packer insisted that the couple had loitered in the street for more than half an hour and that he had watched them eating the grapes in the rain. By 12:15 am the couple had moved across the road and stood in front of the Berner Street Club, listening to the singing. After that Packer, who had begun shutting up shop for the night, lost sight of them.

Further enquiries by the intrepid Grande and Batchelor turned up two sisters, Mrs Rosenfield and Mrs Eva Harstein, of 14 Berner Street, who both claimed to have seen some flower petals and a bloodied grape stalk close to where the body of Elizabeth Stride had been found. The two detectives therefore headed over to Dutfield's Yard and on searching the drain they are said to have discovered a grape stalk.

The police were more than a little perturbed by Matthew Packer's sudden recollection – especially by the fact that the subsequent article in the *Evening News* ended with the reporter's observation, 'Well, Mr Packer, I suppose the police came at once to ask you and your wife what you knew about the affair, as soon as ever the body was discovered?'

'The Police', Packer was reported to have contemptuously replied. 'No they haven't asked me a word about it yet!'

Sergeant White was promptly dispatched to reinterview this now seemingly important witness. When he got to the shop, Mrs Packer told him that her husband had been taken to the mortuary by the two private detectives. White headed off again, and met Packer returning with one of the detectives. He asked him where he had been and received the reply that he had been to see if he could identify the woman. White asked him if he had done so.

'Yes', was Packer's reply, 'I believe she bought some grapes at my shop at about 12 o'clock on Saturday'.

Later that day, Grand and Batchelor took Packer to Scotland Yard where he was personally interviewed by Sir Charles Warren. This time he claimed to have sold the grapes to the couple an hour earlier – at 11 pm – and to have then closed his shop, leaving the couple standing in the street.

It is, of course, possible that he had misremembered the time. But what is noticeable about Packer's various statements is that they were constantly evolving, with more details and embellishments being added over the days that followed. Several of these blatantly drew on newspaper reports and popular gossip, as more and more details about Elizabeth Stride's appearance and clothing at the time of her death were sought out and published by journalists. Perhaps Packer was another person who was enjoying his time in the limelight, and was telling his interviewers the facts he thought they wished to hear. Or perhaps the prospect of the £500 reward offered by the City Police for information that might lead to the apprehension of the killer proved too much of an allure for a hardworking Whitechapel greengrocer, and he began fabricating his story in the hope that, should even part of it prove correct, he would be entitled to a share of it. In Packer's defence, it must be said that several of his facts remained consistent with each retelling of the story. But his different statements also contained numerous inconsistencies, not to mention outright inaccuracies, and these, according to Chief Inspector Swanson, reporting on the murder to the Home Office on October 19th, were sufficient to render 'any statement he made… almost valueless as evidence'.

At the subsequent inquest, Dr. George Bagster Phillips was adamant that 'the deceased had not swallowed either skin or seed of a grape within many hours of her death'. But local gossips were not easily dissuaded, and several people claimed that Elizabeth Stride had died with a grape stem clenched tightly in her fist. This, when merged with Packer's tale of the well-spoken stranger who bought her grapes shortly before her murder, and the subsequent coverage of his story in the newspapers, ensured that the grapes soon became an integral part of the Jack the Ripper legend. Thus the idea of an upper class killer luring his hapless victims (such a dramatic image could never be confined to just one victim) to their deaths by dangling a bunch of grapes in front of them took root. It has been doing the rounds ever since. Successive generations have duly contributed their own embellishments, with several recent films and television dramatizations making the macabre suggestion that the grapes were adulterated with a powerful narcotic to render the victims unconscious before Dr. Jack or Sir Jack commenced his mutilations.

Mrs Fanny Mortimer, who lived at 36 Berner Street, four doors up from Dutfield's Yard, proved a somewhat more consistent witness. Nonetheless, her experience gave rise to an even more widespread yet equally erroneous image of the Ripper. She told of how around 12:30 am, she had heard 'the measured, heavy stamp of a policeman passing her house on his beat'. For some reason, she had then gone out into the street and stood outside her door for a while. Then she went back indoors, and was getting ready for bed when she heard a terrible commotion. She ran outside again and was informed that there had been another dreadful murder. Entering Dutfield's Yard, she saw the body of a woman, 'lying huddled up just inside the gates with her throat cut from ear to ear'. She later recalled that no noise had been made, and that she did not observe anyone enter the gates during her time outside. The only man she had seen in Berner Street was a young man who was carrying a black shiny bag. Later that day, she told the *Daily News* how he 'walked very fast down the street from the direction of Commercial Road…looked up at the club, and then went round the corner by the Board School'. She also gave it as her opinion that, 'If a man had come out of the yard before one o'clock I must [as in would] have seen him…' Her statement received widespread publicity and was greatly embellished in the months and even years that followed. Reminiscing in his memoirs some 50 years later, Walter Dew credited Mrs Mortimer with being 'the only person ever to see the Ripper in the vicinity of one of his crimes'. According to Dew's account, she was about to re-enter her cottage when she heard the approach of Diemshutz's horse and cart.

> At the same moment [she] observed something else, silent and sinister. A man, whom she judged to be about thirty, dressed in black, carrying a small, shiny black bag, hurried furtively along the opposite side of the court... The man had been so quiet that she had not seen him until he was abreast of her. His head was turned away, as though he did not wish to be seen.

It seems evident that Walter Dew was either misremembering or had been influenced by later embellishments of this widely circulated story. Furthermore it would appear that he was not kept particularly well informed by his superiors, for Mrs Mortimer had most definitely not seen 'the Ripper in the vicinity of one of his crimes'. Leon Goldstein was horrified when he heard local gossip about the suspicious-looking man seen hurrying away from the scene of the murder. He had, he told the police when he walked into Leman Street Police Station the next day, left a coffee house in Spectacle Alley only a short time before Mrs Mortimer's sighting, and had indeed hurried past her carrying a bag full of empty cigarette boxes on his way home to 22 Christian Street.

Goldstein was not in any way related to the crime, and was most certainly not the Whitechapel murderer. Yet his hasty dash home along Berner Street would furnish the killer with one of his most readily recognizable features. For although Mrs Mortimer's sighting of him received widespread press coverage, his self-identification and subsequent absolution by the police did not, and the shiny black bag became as integral a part of the murderer's reputed paraphernalia as the top hat and swirling cape.

Thus the image of the murderer as an upper class 'toff' began to take shape, and when, a few days after the double murder, the police released a letter written in an educated hand, and bearing the chilling, yet gruesomely accurate, sobriquet 'Jack the Ripper', a legend was well and truly born.

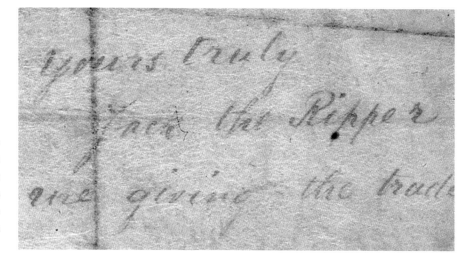

RIGHT: It was the signature on a letter that had been handed to the police on September 29th that gave the Whitechapel Murder the now infamous name Jack the Ripper.

CHAPTER ELEVEN

The Murder of Catherine Eddowes

At almost exactly the same time as the discovery of Elizabeth Stride's body in Dutfield's Yard, another prostitute named Catherine or 'Kate' Eddowes was being released from Bishopsgate Police Station in the City of London. At around 8:30 pm that evening, she had been entertaining a delighted crowd of onlookers outside 29 Aldgate High Street with a spontaneous, though drunken, imitation of a fire engine. Having taken a bow, she lay down on the pavement and went to sleep. PC Robinson of the City Police arrived on the scene and asked if any of the onlookers knew who she was or where she lived. None of them did. So Robinson hauled her to her feet and leant her against the wall. She promptly slid back down onto the pavement. Robinson summoned a colleague, PC George Simmons, and together they manhandled her round to Bishopsgate Police Station. Here, when asked her name, Kate replied, 'Nothing'. The officers placed her in a cell and left her to sober up. She had soon fallen into a comatose sleep.

PC George Hutt, the city jailor, came on duty at 10 pm and took over responsibility for the prisoners in the cells. He checked on her several times over the next few hours, and found her fast asleep. By 12:15 am she had woken and Hutt heard her singing softly. Quarter of an hour later she called to him and asked when she would be allowed to leave.

'When you can take care of yourself', Hutt called back.

'I can do that now', came her reply.

At 12:55 am he brought her from the cell and told her she could go. He pushed open the swing door to the passage and said, 'This way Missus'.

As she walked to the outer door, she asked him what time it was.

'Too late for you to get any more drink', observed Hutt.

'I shall get a damned fine hiding when I get home', she sighed.

Hutt was not in the least bit sympathetic. 'And serve you right', he replied, 'you have no right to get drunk'.

As Kate left the station, Hutt asked her to shut the door behind her.

'All right', she chirped, 'Good night, old cock'.

So saying, she turned left and headed off towards Houndsditch. According to Hutt's later estimation, it would have taken her around eight minutes' 'ordinary walking' to reach Mitre Square, during which time the murderer of Elizabeth Stride was also heading toward the square from the opposite direction.

Mitre Square, situated about half a mile to the west of Berner Street, lay just inside the City of London boundary. It was then an enclosed square over which towered three imposing warehouse buildings. Three

OPPOSITE: These cobblestones are all that remains of the Mitre Square, where the body of Catherine Eddowes was found in the early hours of September 30th, 1888. The exact site is now occupied by a flower bed.

ABOVE: According to the doctor who examined her at the scene of her murder, the corner where the body of Catherine Eddowes was discovered was the darkest part of Mitre Square.

uninhabited houses and a shop backed onto its south-west corner, while two more houses, one of which was occupied by a city policeman, Richard Pearse, nestled between the warehouses. The square was bordered by Mitre Street to the west, Aldgate High Street to the south, and Duke's Place to the east. Nearby, on Bevis Marks, stood the Great Synagogue. The church of St Botolph was a stone's throw away, with the south side of Aldgate High Street beyond, lined with butchers' shops and slaughterhouses, and consequently known as Butcher's Row. There were three entrances to the square – a fairly wide one that came in from Mitre Street; the narrower St James's Place (known locally as the Orange Market) in the north-east corner; and the long, narrow Church Passage in the south-east corner that came in from Duke's Place.

At 1:30 am PC Watkins of the City Police passed this south-east corner on a beat that brought him through Mitre Square every 12–14 minutes. He had his lantern on, fixed to his belt. He was later emphatic that the square had been quite deserted and that no one could have been hiding there without him seeing them. He left the square and turned right toward Aldgate.

Five minutes later, three Jewish gentlemen, Harry Harris, Joseph Hyam Levy, and Joseph Lawende left the Imperial Club on Duke's Place and, as they passed its junction with Church Passage, noticed a man and woman talking quietly together. The woman had her back to them, but they could see that her hand was resting on the man's chest. Levy was immediately convinced that the couple were up to no good, and announced brusquely, 'I don't like going home by myself when I see these sorts of characters about'. In his hurry to get away he paid the couple scant attention and was unable to furnish a description of either of them, although he did say that the man may have been about 3 inches taller than the woman.

Joseph Lawende, however, was a little less disgusted and a little more observant. Although he hadn't actually seen the woman's face, he was almost certain, when later shown it at the police station, that her clothing was that worn by Catherine Eddowes. Although the street lighting wasn't particularly good, he did catch a brief glimpse of the man's face and was able to provide a description.

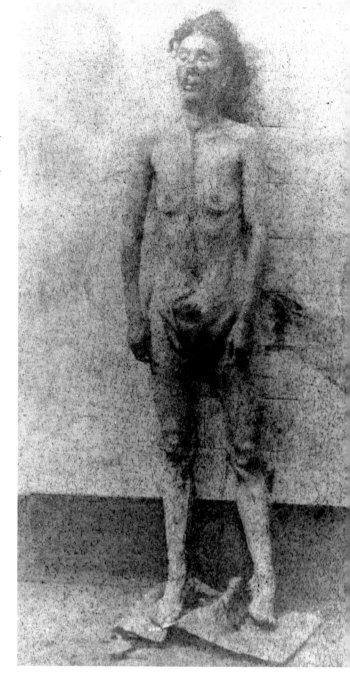

He had the appearance of a sailor and was aged about 30. He was around 5 feet 9 inches tall, of medium build, had a fair complexion, and a small fair moustache. He sported a reddish neckerchief tied in a knot, wore a pepper-and-salt coloured loose-fitting jacket, and had on a grey peaked cloth cap. However, it should be noted that Lawende caught only a quick glimpse of the man as he passed by, and since the couple were doing nothing particularly suspicious, he later maintained that he would not be able to recognize or identify the man were he to see him again.

At 1:44 am PC Watkins turned out of Leadenhall Street, strolled along Mitre Street, and veered right into Mitre Square. Almost immediately he saw a sight that sent him reeling back in horror. Catherine Eddowes was lying on her back in a pool of blood, with her clothes thrown up over her waist. This time the killer had targeted the face. There was a cut through her lower left eyelid and a scratch through the skin on the upper left eyelid near to the angle of the nose. The right eyelid had been similarly cut. Deep triangular cuts had been carved into her cheeks. There was a deep cut over the bridge of the nose, the tip of which had been sliced off. The lobes of her ears had been nicked and her throat had been cut back to the spine. Once more horrific abdominal injuries had occurred. A knife had been thrust into the lower abdomen, ripping her open. The liver had been stabbed and both the uterus and the left kidney were missing from the body.

Racing across the square, Watkins burst into Kearley and Tonge's warehouse where he knew that a retired policeman, George Morris, was working as a night watchman. 'For God's sake, mate!' cried Watkins. 'Come to my assistance… Here is another woman cut to pieces!'

Pausing to get his lamp, the night watchman followed Watkins to the square's south-west corner, took one look at the body, and raced off along Mitre Street towards Aldgate, blowing furiously on his whistle as he ran. In Aldgate he met PC James Harvey and PC Holland and brought them back to the square. Holland went immediately to fetch Dr. George Sequira from his abode on nearby Jewry Street.

Sequira was at the scene by 1:55 am and later told the inquest that the murder had occurred in what was probably the darkest part of Mitre Square, although there had certainly been enough light for the miscreant to perpetrate the deed. Death, he said, would have been instantaneous once the murderer had cut the windpipe and the blood vessels. Significantly, he was of the opinion that the murderer possessed no great anatomical skill – in other words, he had only a basic knowledge of anatomy – and when asked by the coroner if he would have expected the murderer to be spattered with blood, replied, 'Not necessarily'.

However, at the scene of the murder in the early hours of that morning, Sequira did little more than pronounce life extinct and decided not to touch the body, preferring instead to await the arrival of the City Police Divisional Surgeon, Dr. Frederick Gordon Brown.

Police officers were soon converging on Mitre Square from all over the City. Inspector Edward Collard arrived from Bishopsgate Police Station and ordered an immediate search of the neighborhood, instructing that door-to-door inquiries were to be made around Mitre Square. Next on the scene was Superintendent James McWilliam, head of the City Police Detective Department, who arrived with a number of detectives, all of whom he sent off to make a thorough search of the Spitalfields streets and lodging houses.

As the officers began to fan out through the streets, several men were stopped and questioned, but to no avail. The killer, it appeared, had simply melted away into the darkness. It is probable that he made his escape via the adjacent St James's Place, where there was a Metropolitan fire escape station. Yet the firemen on duty had seen and heard nothing at all. Neither had City Police Constable Richard Pearse who lived at 3 Mitre Square, where his bedroom window looked across at the murder site. George Morris, the night watchman, whose whistle had first alerted the police at large to the atrocity, expressed himself totally baffled as to how such a brutal crime could have been committed close by, without him hearing a sound. As the *Illustrated Police News* reported:

BELOW: It was through the archway in the corner of Mitre Square that Catherine Eddowes killer probably made his escape.

He could hear the footsteps of the policeman as he passed on his beat every quarter of an hour, so that it appeared impossible that the woman could have uttered any sound without his detecting it. It was only on the night that he remarked to some policeman that he wished the 'butcher' would come round Mitre Square and he would give him a doing; yet the 'butcher' had come and he was perfectly ignorant of it.

Stranger still, at the exact moment that Catherine Eddowes was entering Mitre Square with her murderer, three City detectives, Daniel Halse, Robert Outram, and Edward Marriot, were busily orchestrating plain clothes patrols of the City's eastern fringe. Yet the murderer had managed to slip past them undetected.

Halse was over by St Botolph's Church when he learned of the murder just before 2 am. Hurrying to Mitre Square, he gave instructions to the constables present to search the neighbourhood. He then set off to make his own search, heading first to Middlesex Street and from there to Wentworth Street, where he stopped to question two men. Both were able to give him a satisfactory account of their movements and he allowed them to continue on their way. He then passed through Goulston Street at around 2:20 am, where he noticed nothing untoward, and headed back to Mitre Square. Here he found that the body had been removed to the Golden Lane Mortuary. On his way there, he learnt that a portion of the deceased's apron was missing, and was presumed to have been taken by her killer.

At around 2:55 am PC Alfred Long of the Metropolitan Police, one of the extra constables drafted into the area after the Annie Chapman murder, was walking his beat along Goulston Street. As he passed the doorway that led to the staircases of 108–119 Wentworth Model Dwellings, he found the missing portion of the woman's apron. It was stained with blood and faeces, one section of it was wet, and the blade of a knife had apparently been wiped on it. Long had earlier passed that way at roughly 2:20 am, about the same time as Halse, but like the City detective, he too had seen nothing to attract his attention. Indeed he was sure that the fragment had not been there then.

The piece of bloodstained apron was the only clue that the killer ever left behind. Firstly it tells us which way he was heading. Having murdered twice in less than an hour he had to be going to ground, so the location of the apron suggests someone who lived to the east of Mitre Square.

The apron also answers a fundamental question about how the killer would have appeared after such gruesome murders. It is commonly believed that he must have been drenched in blood. Even if this was so, it was not unusual to see people in bloodstained clothing in the early hours, since there were 80 or so butchers and slaughterhouses in the district whose employees worked through the night. But the evidence suggests that Jack the Ripper asphyxiated his victims before he commenced his mutilations, so by the time he cut their throats, their hearts had all but stopped beating. Therefore there would not necessarily have been an arterial spurt to cover him in blood. Moreover, his victims were all prostitutes and when they went with him into the dark corners of squares and passageways, they were only doing so for one reason. Suppose that when he met them he was wearing a buttoned-up overcoat, which he took off before committing the murders? He could have had blood all over his shirt, jacket, and trousers, but by putting the coat back on he would have covered the bloodstains. His hands, as is clear from the state of the apron, must also have been covered in blood and he would, no doubt, have wanted to wipe them clean as quickly as possible after his escape from Mitre Square. But had he done so in the streets this might have attracted attention and suspicion; he needed a shielded place in which to clean himself up, and the dark, recessed doorway in Goulston Street, evidently offered sufficient cover for him to do so quickly and safely. Once clear of any visible incriminating bloodstains, he simply dropped the apron in the doorway and continued on his way.

Long's first thought on discovering the portion of apron was that someone may have been attacked and could at that very moment be lying injured or dead on a staircase or landing inside the dwellings. So he stood up, intending to search the block. As he did so, he noticed a scrawled chalk message on the wall directly above the apron, which read, 'The Juwes are the men that will not be blamed for nothing'. Moments later another officer arrived at the scene, and Long asked him to guard the building – telling

BELOW: It was in a doorway of Wentworth Model Dwellings, the large building on the right of the photograph, that Jack the Ripper left his only clue.

him to keep a careful watch on anybody entering or leaving it – while he took the portion of apron round to Commercial Street Police Station and handed it over to an inspector.

Soon, officers of the Metropolitan Police were gathering around the doorway and were gazing at the graffiti with great trepidation. Mindful of the anti-Semitism that had surfaced in the area in the wake of the Leather Apron scare, and realizing that Wentworth Model Dwellings not only stood in a largely Jewish locality but were also inhabited almost exclusively by Jews, the Metropolitan Police began to fear that if the message was left it could lead to a resurgence of racial unrest in the district, with dire consequences. They were therefore anxious to erase the message sooner rather than later. But both the portion of apron and the graffiti pertained to a murder investigation being carried out by the City Police, detectives from which had soon crossed the boundary and were also gathering around the doorway. They were not so keen to erase what they saw as an important clue, and the two forces clashed over what should be done. The City Police were adamant that it should be photographed. The Metropolitan Police pointed out that this would mean waiting until it was light, by which time Gentiles would be arriving in their thousands to purchase from the Jewish stallholders at Petticoat Lane and Goulston Street Sunday markets. Since there was no way of keeping it hidden from these crowds, the Metropolitan Police feared that a full-scale anti-Jewish riot might result. Daniel Halse suggested a compromise whereby only the top line, 'The Juwes are', would be erased. But, as Superintendent Arnold, of the Metropolitan Police, later pointed out in a report, 'Had only a portion of the writing been removed the context would have remained'.

The bickering was still going on when Sir Charles Warren arrived at the scene between 5 am and 5:30 am. Because the doorway stood on Metropolitan Police territory, his word was final, and he immediately concurred with his officers that leaving the graffiti any longer would almost certainly lead to far greater crimes against innocent Jews. So he ordered that the message be erased without delay, and before any photograph of it could be taken. It would prove the most controversial order he gave in the entire investigation: Major Smith, the acting City Police Commissioner, considered it a huge blunder and could barely disguise his contempt for Warren's actions in the days and weeks that followed.

On November 6th, in a report to the Home Office, Warren defended his action:

It was just getting light, the public would be in the streets in a few minutes, in a neighbourhood very much crowded by Jewish vendors and Christian Purchasers from all parts of London... The writing was on the jamb of the open archway or doorway visible to anybody in the street and could not be covered up without danger of the covering been torn off at once. A discussion took place whether the writing could be left covered up or otherwise... for an hour until it could be photographed; but after taking into consideration the excited state of the population in London...the strong feeling which had been excited against the Jews, and the fact that in a short time there would be a large concourse of the people in the streets, and having before me a report that if it was left there the house was likely to be wrecked (in which from my own observation I entirely concurred) I considered it desirable to obliterate the writing at once... I do not hesitate to say that if the writing had been left there would have been an onslaught upon the Jews, property would have been wrecked, and lives would probably have been lost...

Given the racial unrest that the 'Leather Apron' scare had generated in the area, the fears of the Metropolitan Police were probably justified. Erasing the graffiti, however questionable in the eyes of conspiracy theorists, probably did prevent the mob from once more venting their anger on innocent Jewish scapegoats.

CHAPTER TWELVE

YOURS TRULY, JACK THE RIPPER

I'm not a butcher, I'm not a Yid,
Nor yet a foreign skipper,
But I'm your own light-hearted friend,
Yours truly, Jack the Ripper.
Anon.

The days following the double murder saw one of the most significant developments in the hunt for the killer. The fact that two women had been brutally slain within an hour of each other, apparently by the same man, only a short distance apart, ensured that public fear and fascination was raised to a whole new level. As word of a 'double event' crackled around the metropolis, excited and agitated crowds flocked to the murder sites to speculate on the killer's motives and identity. Berner Street was said to have been packed with a sea of heads from end to end. The thoroughfares around Mitre Square were blocked by ghoulish spectators. The murders were rapidly assuming a distinct air of melodrama, and on October 1st the actions of the Metropolitan Police saw to it that the gruesome pantomime was given a villain, who would ensure that it would run and run.

On September 29th, 1888, the Central News Agency, whose offices were situated on New Bridge Street in the City of London, forwarded a letter to the police that they had received on September 27th. The missive, dated September 25th, was addressed to 'The Boss, Central News Office, London, City'. It read:

Dear Boss,
I keep on hearing the police have caught me but they wont fix me just yet. I have laughed when they look so clever and talk about being on the right track. That joke about Leather Apron gave me real fits. I am down on whores and I shant quit ripping them till I do get buckled. Grand work the last job was. I gave the lady no time to squeal. How can they catch me now. I love my work and want to start again. You will soon hear of me with my funny little games. I saved some of the proper red stuff in a ginger beer bottle over the last job to write with but it went thick like glue and I cant use it. Red ink is fit enough I hope ha. ha. The next job I do I shall clip the ladys ears off and send to the police officers just for jolly wouldn't you. Keep this letter back till I do a bit more work, then give it out straight. My knife's so nice and sharp I want to get to work right away if I get a chance. Good Luck.
Yours truly
Jack the Ripper
Dont mind me giving the trade name
Wasnt good enough to post this before I got all the red ink off my hands curse it No luck yet. They say I'm a doctor now. ha ha

OPPOSITE: It was this now infamous letter received by the Central News Office on September 27th that gave Jack the Ripper his name.

2₅ Sept. 1888.

Dear Boss.

I keep on hearing the police have caught me. but they wont fix me just yet. I have laughed when they look so clever and talk about being on the right track. That joke about Leather Apron gave me real fits. I am down on whores and I shant quit ripping them till I do get buckled. Grand work the last job was. I gave the lady no time to squeal. How can they catch me now. I love my work and want to start again. You will soon hear of me with my funny little games. I saved some of the proper red stuff in a ginger beer bottle over the last job to write with but it went thick like glue and I cant use it. Red ink is fit enough I hope ha. ha. The next job I do I shall clip

At first the police were convinced that the letter was a hoax. But within 24 hours of their receipt of it, the 'double event' occurred, leaving them with little choice but to take an interest in what 'Jack the Ripper' had to say. The comment that 'I want to get to work right away if I get a chance…' gave some credence to the author's claim to be the murderer; while his threat to 'clip the ladys ears off and send to the police officers' was now, so the police thought, far too prophetic to dismiss as an empty boast. Furthermore, their investigation was rapidly losing both momentum and direction, and they were in desperate need of a breakthrough. Perhaps the 'Dear Boss' missive could provide it?

So, on October 1st, the letter and its contents were made public, and from that moment on, five sordid East End murders were guaranteed a gruesome immortality, and the homicidal miscreant responsible would enter the realm of legend.

In the early post on Monday October 1st, a postcard written in handwriting similar to that of the 'Dear Boss' letter was delivered to the Central News Agency. Again written in red ink, and this time stained with what appeared to be blood, the postcard was undated by the author but was stamped with a LONDON

BELOW: This postcard, sent to the Central News Office in the immediate aftermath of the 'Double Event', appeared to show that the author possessed detailed knowledge of the killings.

E postmark dated October 1st. If the writer was not the same person behind the original communiqué, he was most certainly familiar with its contents:

I was not codding dear old Boss when I gave you the tip, you'll hear about Saucy Jacky's work tomorrow double event this time number one squealed a bit couldn't finish straight off. had not the time to get ears for police. thanks for keeping last letter back till I got to work again.
Jack the Ripper

The inference of the postcard was, of course, that it had been written within hours of the murders, and that the author was informing the police of the two killings he had just committed. Furthermore it boasted that he had indeed attempted to make good his promise to 'clip the ears' off a victim. Whether or not the police believed it to come from the murderer was largely immaterial; the correspondence had to be investigated and, if possible, its author traced, if only to eliminate him as a suspect. So both the card and the 'Dear Boss' letter were reproduced on posters, which were placed outside police stations with a request for anyone recognizing the handwriting to contact the police. By October 4th facsimiles had been released to the press and were beginning to appear in newspapers all over the world. Encouraged by this widespread publicity, hoaxers across the country began reaching for their pens, and the beleaguered detectives were soon inundated with Jack the Ripper correspondence. All of it had to be read, assessed and, if possible, its writers investigated. As the journalist George Simms observed in his 'Dragnet' column, for the *Referee*, on Sunday October 7th:

JACK THE RIPPER is the hero of the hour. A gruesome wag, a grim practical joker, has succeeded in getting an enormous amount of fun out of a postcard which he sent to the Central News. The fun is all his own, and nobody shares in it, but he must be gloating demonically at the present moment at the state of perturbation in which he has flung the public mind. Grave journals have reproduced the sorry jest, and have attempted to seriously argue that the awful Whitechapel fiend is the idle and mischievous idiot who sends blood-stained postcards to the news agency. Of course the whole business is a farce.

The police appear to have realized early on, if they were ever in any doubt of the fact, that the letter and postcard were not the work of the Whitechapel murderer. On October 10th Sir Charles Warren informed the Home Office, 'At present I think the whole thing a hoax but of course we are bound to try & ascertain the writer in any case'. Robert Anderson, when serializing his memoirs prior to their publication in 1910, was even more adamant that the letter was a hoax, and even went so far as to suggest that the police were aware of the prankster's identity:

I will only add here that the 'Jack the Ripper' letter which is preserved in the Police Museum at New Scotland Yard is the creation of an enterprising London Journalist.

Indeed the fact that the sender had the wherewithal to send his communication to a news agency, as opposed to a local or national newspaper, suggests that he did indeed have an in-depth knowledge of how the press worked. As George Simms observed:

The fact that the self-postcard-proclaimed assassin sent his imitation blood-besmeared communication to the Central News people opens up a wide field for theory. How many among you, my dear readers, would have hit upon the idea of 'the Central News' as a receptacle for your confidence? You might have sent your joke to the *Telegraph, The Times,* any morning or any evening paper, but I will lay long odds that it would never have occurred to communicate with a Press agency. Curious, is it not, that this maniac makes his communication to an agency which serves the entire Press? It is an idea which might occur to a Pressman perhaps; and even then it would probably only occur to someone connected with the editorial department of a newspaper, someone who knew what the Central News was, and the place it filled in the business of news supply. This proceeding on Jack's part betrays an inner knowledge of the newspaper world which is certainly surprising. Everything therefore points to the fact that the jokist is professionally connected with the Press. And if he is telling the truth and not fooling us, then we are brought face to face with the fact that the Whitechapel murders have been committed by a practical journalist - perhaps by a real live editor! Which is absurd, and at that I think I will leave it.

In 1913, retired Detective Chief Inspector John George Littlechild, who at the time of the murders was head of Special Branch and therefore privy to much of the contemporary opinion among senior officers on the case, replied to a query sent to him by George Simms about the 'Dear Boss' letter. According to Littlechild, the missive was actually composed by either Thomas Bulling, who worked for the Central News Agency, or John Moore, who was its manager.

Another alleged creator of the name Jack the Ripper was a journalist known simply as Best, who at the time of the murders was supposedly working as a freelance reporter for the Star newspaper. He allegedly confessed in 1931 that he and a 'provincial colleague' had written all the Jack the Ripper letters in order to 'keep the business alive'. However, it is difficult to ascertain the veracity of Best's confession, and given that the Jack the Ripper letters run into hundreds and are in many styles of handwriting, Best and his provincial colleague must have been master forgers to accomplish the calligraphic differences displayed in all of them!

Bulling seems the more credible choice. It was he who forwarded a third letter to the police, which was dated October 5th and which again purported to come from 'Jack the Ripper'. He enclosed the envelope that contained the letter and observed that it was 'in the same handwriting as the previous communications'. But, interestingly, he only sent a handwritten copy of the original. Perhaps he was finding it difficult to disguise his handwriting? The letter included several biblical quotes and more threats such as, 'I must get to work tomorrow treble event this time yes yes three must be ripped. will send you a bit of face by post I promise this dear old Boss'. The letter ended with the taunt, 'The police now reckon my work a practical joke well well Jacky's a very practical joker ha ha Keep this back till three are wiped out and you can show the cold meat'.

Obviously, whether it was either Bulling or Best who invented the name 'Jack the Ripper' will now never be ascertained. What is interesting about this third letter, however, is that by October 5th the police were evidently dubious about its origin and were beginning to realize that releasing the letters had hindered rather than helped their investigation. Indeed it seems likely that they asked the Central News Agency not to release the details, and as a result it was hardly mentioned in the newspapers.

Only one author of a Jack the Ripper missive was ever prosecuted by the authorities. At Bradford Borough Court on October 19th, a Canadian-born milliner and dressmaker, Maria Coroner of 13 Westgrove Street, Bradford, described by the newspapers as 'a respectable looking young woman aged twenty one years of age', was charged with having 'written certain letters tending to cause a breach of the peace'. Maria had written two letters, one to the Chief Constable and the other to a local newspaper. Both were signed 'Jack the Ripper' and spoke of his intention to visit Bradford and 'do a little business' before starting to some other place on the 'same errand'. In court she excused her 'foolish conduct' by saying that she 'had done it

as a joke'. The magistrate didn't see the funny side and remanded her in custody.

When she next appeared, on October 23rd, 'a dense crowd fought for admission to the court'. According to the *Star*, 'The prisoner listened to the proceedings with an amused expression'. She was fined £20 and bound over to keep the peace for six months, being told that if she 'again transgressed she would go to gaol'. Doubtless many of the sickest and most perverted sentiments expressed in the Jack the Ripper correspondence were written by similarly 'respectable' Victorian citizens who found the titillation offered by the press reportage of the murders irresistible.

At around the time that Maria Coroner was composing her prank missives, somewhere in London another anonymous correspondent was preparing to make good a threat that had appeared in virtually all the letters received in early October – the threat to send a body part in the mail.

George Lusk, president of the Mile End Vigilance Committee, had been extremely busy throughout early October. In addition to gathering information from local informants, he was also addressing meetings and liaising with the press. He had also been badgering both the Home Office and Queen Victoria to offer a reward for information that might lead to the apprehension of the killer. His name was therefore frequently mentioned in the press. Several people appear to have taken an interest in him and he soon attracted what would today be known as a stalker, possibly even two.

On Thursday October 4th at 4:15 pm, a man of around 30–40 years of age, 5 feet 9 inches tall, of florid complexion with a bushy brown beard, whiskers, and moustache, went to the private residence of Mr Lusk in Alderney Street, Mile End, and asked for him. He happened to be at a tavern kept by his son, and thither the man went. After asking all sorts of questions about the beats taken by members of the committee, the man 'attempted to induce Mr Lusk to enter a private room with him'. According to the *News of The World*:

> The stranger's appearance however was so repulsive and forbidding that Mr Lusk declined, but consented to hold a quiet conversation with him in the bar-parlour. The two were talking, when the stranger drew a pencil from his pocket and purposely dropped it over the side of the table saying, 'Pick that up'. Just as Mr Lusk turned to do so he noticed the stranger make a swift though silent movement of his right hand towards his side pocket, and seeing that he was detected assumed a nonchalant air, and asked to be directed to the nearest coffee and dining-rooms. Mr Lusk directed him to a house in the Mile End-road, and the stranger quietly left the house, followed by Mr Lusk who went to the coffee-house indicated, and found that the man

had not been there, but had given his pursuer the slip by disappearing up a court.

Mr George Lusk's vigilance activities had, it seems, made him a magnet for all manner of sinister characters and sick individuals. On October 10th another suspicious-looking man was seen lurking outside his house. This time Lusk reported him to the police and a description was circulated. On October 12th, Lusk was targetted by one of the Jack the Ripper correspondents and received a letter in handwriting supposedly similar to that of the 'Dear Boss' letter. It read:

> I write you a letter in black ink, as I have no more of the right stuff. I think you are all asleep in Scotland-yard with your bloodhounds, as I will show you to-morrow night (Saturday). I am going to do a double Event, but not in Whitechapel. Got rather too warm there. Had to shift. No more till you hear me again.
> JACK THE RIPPER.

Naturally George Lusk was beginning to fear for his personal safety, and no doubt that of his family, when yet another postcard addressed to 'Mr Lusk, Head Vigilance Committee, Alderney-street, Mile End' arrived to taunt him still further:

> Say Boss -
> You seem rare frightened, guess I'd like to give you fits, but can't stop time enough to let your box of toys play copper games with me, but hope to see you when I don't hurry much
> Bye Bye Boss.

On October 15th a Miss Marsh was behind the counter in her father's leather shop, at 218 Jubilee Street, a short distance from the London Hospital, when a man dressed like a cleric entered. He wanted to know about the vigilance committee's reward poster in the shop window and asked if she knew the address of Mr George Lusk. She suggested he enquire at the nearby Crown, but the man insisted he didn't want to go to a pub. Obligingly she got out a newspaper that gave Lusk's street address, although not his house number, and read it out to the stranger who proceeded to take it down in a notebook. Miss Marsh described the man as being around 45 years old, 6 feet tall, of slim build with a sallow complexion, dark beard, and moustache. He spoke with what she took to be an Irish brogue. No one answering that description actually called on Lusk, but on the evening of Tuesday October 16th a small package, wrapped in brown paper and bearing an indistinct London postmark, was delivered to him in the evening mail. Although addressed to him by name, and to the street in which he lived, it did not give the house number. Opening the package, Lusk was disgusted by the contents, which consisted of a foul-smelling piece of kidney and a letter which read:

> From hell
> Mr Lusk
> Sor
> I send you half the Kidne I took from one women prasarved it for you tother piece I fried and ate it was very nise I may send you the bloody knif that took it out if you only wate a whil longer
> signed Catch me when you Can
> Mishter Lusk

The handwriting was identical to that on the postcard Lusk had received a few days before. Lusk's first thought was that it was just another sick joke, and he assumed the kidney to be from a sheep or some other animal. However, he decided to seek the opinion of his fellow vigilance committee members, and they were not so sure. They therefore decided to obtain a medical opinion as to whether the kidney was human or animal.

It was duly taken to the Mile End Road surgery of Dr. Frederick Wiles where, in the absence of Wiles himself, his assistant Dr. Reed examined it and immediately pronounced it human. Reed then sought a second opinion at the nearby London Hospital, where he asked the Pathological Curator Dr. Thomas Openshaw to examine the organ. According to the Star, 'By use of the microscope Dr. Openshaw was able to determine that the kidney had been taken from a full-grown human being, and that the portion before him was part of the left kidney'. The newspaper went on to inform its readers that 'There seems to be no room for doubt that what has been sent to Mr Lusk is part of a human kidney, but nevertheless it may be doubted whether

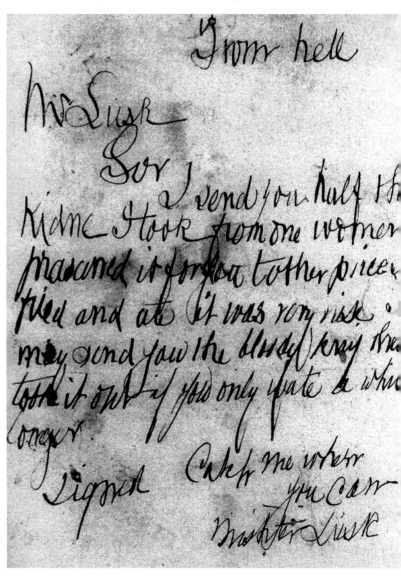

it has any serious bearing on the Mitre-square murder'. Several newspapers, however, quoted Openshaw as having categorically stated that the kidney was that of a woman who had died within the previous three weeks. Openshaw felt a need to refute these claims and in an interview with a *Star* reporter he stated that although he believed it to be half of a left human kidney, he couldn't say whether it was that of a woman, nor how long ago it had been removed from the body, as it had been preserved in spirits. The newspaper ended this report with the observation that, 'The whole thing may possibly turn out to be a medical student's gruesome joke'.

The possibility that sending the kidney was a medical student's prank appears to have struck the police from the outset. After Openshaw's examination, the organ was taken to Leman Street Police Station and then handed over to the City Police in whose jurisdiction Catherine Eddowes had been murdered. The first police report on the subject was submitted by Inspector James McWilliam of the City Police on

RIGHT: The police received hundreds of letters purporting to come from the murderer. The one that, even today, is most hotly debated is the 'From Hell' letter sent to Mr George Lusk.

October 27th, and commented that:

> The kidney has been examined by Dr. Gordon Brown who is of the opinion that it is human. Every effort is being made to trace the sender, but it is not desirable that publicity should be given to the doctor's opinion, or the steps that are being taken in consequence. It might turn out after all to be the act of a Medical Student who would have no difficulty in obtaining the organ in question.

On November 6th Chief Inspector Swanson, who had met daily with Inspector McWilliam to discuss the matter, forwarded a report to the Home Office in which he stated:

> The result of the combined medical opinion... is that it is the kidney of a human adult, not charged with a fluid, as it would have been in the case of a body handed over for purposes of dissection to an hospital, but rather as it would be in the case where it was taken from the body not so destined. In other words similar kidneys might & could be obtained from any dead person upon whom a post mortem had been made from any cause by students or dissecting room porter.

Today, of course, it is impossible to say whether or not the kidney sent to George Lusk was part of the one taken from Catherine Eddowes' body, and was therefore sent by her murderer. It is perhaps the most debated of all the Jack the Ripper missives, and has been the subject of endless speculation and myth making. The doctors who examined it at the time seem to have thought it a hoax. This also appears to have been the consensus among the police officers investigating the case, with the notable exception of Major Henry Smith, the acting City of London Police Commissioner, who later recalled in his memoirs:

> I made over the kidney to the police surgeon, instructing him to consult with the most eminent men in the Profession, and to send me a report without delay. I give the substance of it. The renal artery is about three inches long. Two inches remained in the corpse, one inch was attached to the kidney. The kidney left in the corpse was in an advanced state of Bright's Disease; the kidney sent me was in an exactly similar state. But what was of far more importance, Mr Sutton, one of the senior surgeons at the London Hospital, whom Gordon Brown asked to meet him and another surgeon in consultation, and who was one of the greatest authorities living on the kidney and its diseases, said he would pledge his reputation that the kidney submitted to them had been put in spirits within a few hours of its removal from the body thus effectually disposing of all hoaxes in connection with it.

Unfortunately no report from Sutton has survived, if there ever was one, and it has to be said that Major Smith's veracity has often been called into doubt. Colleagues remembered him as an entertaining and charming raconteur, but also commented on his ability to play fast and loose with the truth when it suited his story. Indeed, Dr. Brown himself was quoted in the *Star* on October 22nd, 1888 as saying that, 'there is no portion of renal artery adhering to [the kidney], it having been trimmed up, so consequently, there could be no correspondence established between the portion of the body from which it was cut'. In the same article he observed that the kidney exhibited 'no trace of decomposition, when we consider the length of time that has elapsed since the commission of the murder, we come to the conclusion that the possibility is slight of its being a portion of the murdered woman of Mitre Square'.

 Whether or not the kidney was sent to Mr Lusk by the murderer of Catherine Eddowes, its arrival in the investigation provided yet another macabre and gruesome twist to the saga – one which inevitably proved irresistible to the letter writers. Dr. Openshaw's comments to the newspapers ensured that his name became synonymous with the Lusk kidney, and on October 29th he opened his mail to find that some anonymous prankster had decided to honor him with his very own missive:

Old boss you was rite it was the left kidny i was goin to hoperate agin close to you ospitle just as i was going to dror mi nife along of er bloomin throte them cusses of coppers spoilt the game but i guess i wil be on the jobn soon and will send you another bit of innerds
Jack the Ripper
O have you seen the devle with his mikerscope and scalpul a-lookin at a kidney with a slide cocked up.

BELOW: Members of the Mile End Vigilance Committee brought the kidney sent to their president, George Lusk, here to the London Hospital to seek Dr. Openshaw's opinion as to whether or not it had come from the body of Catherine Eddowes.

CHAPTER THIRTEEN

SUSPECTS, SUSPICIONS AND FEAR

There is a very general belief among the local detective force in the East-end that the murderer or murderers are lurking in some of the dangerous dens of the low slums, in close proximity to the scenes of the murders. Among other circumstances which support this theory is that some of the houses supposed to be bolted up for the night are found to have secret strings attached to the bolts, so that the house can be entered by persons who are acquainted with these secrets without delay or noise... Even the cellars in some of the slums are stated to be occupied for sleeping purposes by strange characters who only appear in the streets at night. These dilapidated hovels are unfit for human habitation, and are known to the police to be the hiding places of the most dangerous and desperate characters. The police, it is stated, are contemplating a series of immediate and sudden raids upon these dreadful dens, both in the City and Whitechapel.
Daily News, October 4th, 1888

As the police continued to hunt for suspects, several men came forward to claim responsibility for the killings. The majority were drunk, insane, or both. One such person was William Bull, who was 27 years old and described himself as a medical student at the London Hospital. On the evening of October 3rd, he walked into Bishopsgate Police Station and confessed to the murder in Mitre Square. It was obvious to the police that he was drunk as he told them how he had gone with the woman up a narrow street where he had given her half a crown.

'I shall go mad', he sobbed, clutching his head, 'I have done it, and I must put up with it'.

Police enquiries revealed that no such medical student was known at the London Hospital, and Bull's father, who was described as being 'a most respectable man', testified that his son was at home all Saturday night. In court, a now sober Bull excused his confession by saying that he was 'mad drunk' when he did so. He was remanded in custody pending further enquiries, which evidently exonerated him of any involvement.

On the same night a young sailor approached several of the prostitutes who hung around the docks, only to be suddenly denounced by one of them as the murderer. The cry was taken up by her companions, who chased after him. The panic-stricken sailor had little choice but to seek shelter within King David's Lane Police Station. Word spread around the district that the murderer was in police custody and soon an angry mob had surrounded the station. It took the police several hours to diffuse the situation.

Once again the people of the district were terrified, and chose to stay indoors after nightfall. As in the aftermath of Annie Chapman's murder, the streets were abandoned to patrolling police officers. Prostitutes all over London sought shelter at workhouses or other establishments.

'There was scarcely a female figure to be seen', wrote a *Daily News* reporter, following a late-night wander in the district, 'and the one or two who were visible were evidently taking care to keep within easy reach of friendly doorways. As for the quiet squares and byways of the locality they were absolutely lifeless

OPPOSITE: Much of the area has changed beyond recognition since 1888 but some places, such as this old house in Buxton Street, have survived.

and deserted, and the passing stranger who emerged from a side street into the light of the main road was scanned as curiously as the wayfarer through a remote village.'

On the whole, the keepers of the common lodging houses appear to have become a little more understanding and lenient towards those who could not pay for their night's doss. A local clergyman told a journalist how the prostitutes themselves were also looking out for each other. 'You know these women are very good-natured to each other. They are drawn together by common interests and a common danger, and they will help each other all they can.'

As a consequence, distress amongst the majority of Whitechapel prostitutes was not as great as it might have been throughout October. But there were still some who were forced out onto the streets, and for them every minute of the night must have seemed like an eternity. A *Daily News* reporter met one of them:

'Good heavens! What are we to do?' exclaimed a trembling wretch... 'At one o'clock last night... Mother Morris came down into the kitchen, and she says, 'Now, then, you girls who haven't got your doss money-out you go,' and all of them as hadn't got enough was forced to turn out and go into the streets shuddering at every shadow, and expecting every minute to be murdered. What are we to do?'

On October 5th, in an article that could just as easily have been written in the 21st century, the *Star* lectured its readers for their lack of public spirit:

The moral of the whole business is plain enough. It is poverty which lies at the root of what we perhaps rightly call the social evil, and it is by aiming at the abolition of poverty that we shall cure a variety of woes which we usually set down to an entirely different set of causes.

The Whitechapel murders are indeed a tardy visitation on us for our neglect of obvious social duties, for our hopeless individualism. In a city where very few of us know the names of our next-door neighbours we cannot be surprised that a crafty scoundrel like the Whitechapel murderer should be able to hide his misdeeds. But there is a far more rooted unfriendliness in our so-called Christian society than that which concerns the isolation of neighbour from neighbour. There is the alienation of the rich from the poor; there is that especially un-neighbourly form of dealing which consists in one class abstracting the fruits of the labour of another.

On October 9th Dr. Barnardo wrote to *The Times*, telling how he had actually met Elizabeth Stride a few days before she had been murdered. At the time, Barnardo was campaigning to make it illegal for the keepers of common lodging houses to admit young children. Instead he proposed that special shelters be set up exclusively for minors. He decided to find out firsthand how this would be viewed by that 'class of unhappy women who had no abode but the common lodging house', and so, one night in late September, he visited 32 Flower and Dean Street.

In the kitchen there were many persons, some of them being girls and women of the same unhappy class as that to which poor Elizabeth Stride belonged. The company soon recognized me, and the conversation turned upon the previous murders. The female inmates of the kitchen seemed thoroughly frightened at the dangers to which they were presumably exposed. In an explanatory fashion I put before them the scheme which had suggested itself to my mind, by which children at all events could be saved from the contamination of the common lodging-houses and the streets, and so to some extent the supply cut off which feeds the vast ocean of misery in this great city.

The pathetic part of my story is that my remarks were manifestly followed with deep interest by all the women. Not a single scoffing voice was raised in ridicule or opposition. One poor creature, who had evidently been drinking, exclaimed somewhat bitterly to the following effect: - 'We're all up to no good, and no one cares what becomes of us. Perhaps some of us will be killed next!' And then she added, 'If anybody had helped the likes of us long ago we would never have come to this!'

Impressed by the unusual manner of the people, I could not help noticing their appearance somewhat closely, and I saw how evidently some of them were moved. I have since visited the mortuary in which were lying the remains of the poor woman Stride, and I at once recognized her as one of those who stood around me in the kitchen of the common lodging-house on the occasion of my visit last Wednesday week...

Barnardo was so moved by this first-hand experience that he promptly purchased a property in Flower and Dean Street and converted it into a licensed common lodging house for young girls. From the day it opened, each bunk was filled every night.

Others, however, reacted to the crimes in a far less charitable manner. To some of the men of London, the murderer had become something of a folk hero and several irresponsible pranksters thought it a huge joke to go about imitating him. At around 9:30 pm on October 4th, Mrs Sewell of 2 Pole Street, Stepney Green, was on her way to attend a temperance meeting. As she was passing along Redman's Road, a very dark thoroughfare, a man suddenly sprang out in front of her. She was greatly alarmed, especially when she observed that he was holding a glittering object up against his sleeve.

The man noticed her alarm, and 'as if to ingratiate himself' he said, 'I did not hurt you, missus, did I?'

Just then a young man came by, and the mysterious stranger ran off. 'Did you see what he had in his hand?' said the young man to Mrs Sewell, clearly alarmed.

She replied, 'I saw he had something glittering'.

'Why', said the young man, 'it was a huge knife, a foot long'.

The two followed the man, but failed to track him, and in the pursuit they then lost sight of each other.

The imitators were not a phenomenon exclusive to London. A young woman in Liverpool was walking past Shiel Park in early October when

RIGHT: These women are gossiping outside a common lodging house in Flower and Dean Street, where Dr. Barnardo met with Elizabeth Stride shortly before her murder.

an elderly woman aged about 60 urged her 'most earnestly' not to go into the park. She explained that a few minutes previously she had been resting on one of the park seats when she was accosted by a respectable-looking man dressed in a black coat, light trousers and a soft felt hat. He inquired if she knew of any loose woman in the neighborhood. Then, producing a knife with a long, thin blade, he stated he intended to kill as many women in Liverpool as in London, adding that he would send the ears of the first victim to the editor of the *Liverpool Daily Post*.

Compulsive confessors and reckless pranksters were one thing, but for some the murders were a catalyst for psychological problems, often with tragic consequences. On October 17th, a 40-year-old needlewoman named Sarah Goody of 46 Wilson Street, Stepney, was committed to a lunatic asylum by Thames Magistrates Court. She was convinced that she was being followed by men who watched her movements, and intended either to murder or otherwise harm her. She was so frightened that she could neither eat nor sleep. She could think of nothing else, and had she not been taken into the workhouse she would have committed suicide.

A month earlier, on September 16th, a young butcher named Hennell had cut his throat 'from ear to ear' at his parents' house in Hoxton because he feared that they 'were after him for the Whitechapel murder'. His parents had watched him closely, but when his mother had left the room for a minute, he had taken the opportunity to cut his throat.

The police were obviously no closer to catching the killer than they had been in the wake of Annie Chapman's murder and the beleaguered officers were coming under increasing criticism from the press and public alike. The *Star* went so far as to accuse the entire force of being 'rotten to the core'. The *Daily Telegraph* attacked the 'notorious and shameful shortcomings of the detective department', while the East *London Advertiser* lamented that there was 'no detective force in the proper sense of the word in London at all'. On October 2nd, at a demonstration by the unemployed in Hyde Park, a huge banner expressed the feelings of many Londoners. It read simply 'THE WHITECHAPEL MURDERS. WHERE ARE THE POLICE…[?]'

The police were in fact rigorously pursuing their investigations, but had adopted a policy of guarded secrecy to prevent their lines of enquiry from becoming public knowledge. One of Warren's first actions in the days that followed the double murder was to send extra police into the district. Detectives went around in disguise, some, it is rumoured, even dressed as prostitutes. Door-to-door enquiries were made at common lodging houses, in which 2,000 lodgers were questioned and 80,000 handbills were distributed. They read:

> Police Notice. - To the Occupier. - On the mornings of Friday, 31st August, Saturday, 8th, and Sunday, 30th Sept., 1888, women were murdered in Whitechapel, it is supposed by some one residing in the immediate neighbourhood. Should you know of any person to whom suspicion is attached, you are earnestly requested to communicate at once with the nearest police-station. - Metropolitan Police Office, 30th Sept., 1888.

More gruesomely, 76 butchers and slaughterhouses were visited and the characters of their employees ascertained. Many officers found this a particularly difficult task and the horror of the sights and smells remained with them for years. Sailors in the nearby docks were also questioned. On October 13th, the police began a massive search of some of the area's worst slums. For almost a week, officers entered every room of every house. They searched under the beds and looked inside the cupboards. They scrutinized every knife they could find, and they interviewed hundreds of landlords and their lodgers. But despite the thoroughness of the investigation, the murderer remained at large.

On October 23rd, Dr. Robert Anderson, who had returned from sick leave on October 6th, wrote to the

Home Office and pointed out that one of the main problems faced by the police was the lack of clues at any of the crime scenes:

> That a crime of this kind should have been committed without any clue being supplied by the criminal, is unusual, but that five successive murders should have been committed without our having the slightest clue of any kind is extraordinary, if not unique, in the annals of crime.

One of the more famous and misreported initiatives of the Metropolitan Police – that of using bloodhounds – began at around this time. The suggestion was made by the Home Office to Sir Charles Warren, who was not overly convinced that bloodhounds would be of any use. How could a dog be expected to track the killer without a piece of his clothing or a trace of his blood, he queried – on pavements where people had been walking all night long? Notwithstanding his reservations, trials were held in two London parks and Warren found the results encouraging. Indeed, he was sufficiently impressed to give instructions that, in the event of another murder, the body must not be touched until bloodhounds could be brought and put on the scent.

On the streets of Whitechapel an increased police presence ensured that watchful eyes were kept on the dark courtyards and alleyways of the district. Meanwhile the killer was biding his time, mindful that economic necessity would soon force another victim into his clutches. In the early hours of November 9th, 25-year-old Mary Kelly left her room in Miller's Court, desperate to find the money to clear her rent arrears. At the around same time the murderer was also setting out onto the streets and his bloody finale was about to begin.

BELOW: One idea of how to catch the killer was for bloodhounds to be used.

CHAPTER FOURTEEN

MARY KELLY

The simple truth is, that as long as this murderer, whether he be maniac or not, is cool enough to leave no clue behind him; and as long as he confines his operations to women who make themselves accessories to his escape, his crimes may continue. Unless there were a policeman, not merely in every street, but in every house in Whitechapel, it is impossible to secure the safety against the 'monster' of such women as yesterday's victim. The best hope would be that the scare should at length have gone far enough to prevent these poor creatures taking unknown strangers into dark corners or empty rooms. Then the criminal, rendered desperate by his thirst for blood, may do something which will secure his detection. But as long as these Whitechapel women offer themselves to the slaughterer, and the slaughterer does not lose his head, it is unjust to blame the police for failing to protect them.

The Times, November 10th, 1888

At 25 years old, Mary Kelly was much younger than the other victims of Jack the Ripper. The *Daily Telegraph* described her as being of 'fair complexion, with light hair, and possessing rather attractive features'. Remembering her in his memoirs 50 years later, Walter Dew claimed that he knew her quite well by sight and told of how he had often seen her 'parading along Commercial Street, between Flower and Dean Street and Aldgate, or along Whitechapel Road'. She was, he continued, 'usually in the company

LEFT: Press speculation and sensationalism increased dramatically in the wake of the murder of the Ripper's final victim, Mary Kelly.

OPPOSITE: This shop in Brushfield Street still bears the name of its 1880s' proprietor, Hungarian-Jewish Milliner, Amelia Gold.

42½ A. GOLD *French Milliner* **42**

WHITBREAD'S ALE

OFF-SALES

OPEN

Licensed to Sell Beers, Wines, & Spirits OFF the Premises

UK CHEESES FROM NEALS YARD.

FINE CHOCOLATE ★

A. GOLD ~ Traditional Foods of Britain

of two or three of her kind, fairly neatly dressed and invariably wearing a clean white apron, but no hat'. She appears to have been well liked in the area; the only criticism made by those who knew her was that she was occasionally tipsy.

For the eight months prior to her death, she had been renting a room in Miller's Court off Dorset Street in Spitalfields, and until two weeks before her murder, an unemployed Billingsgate fish porter named Joseph Barnet had been living there with her. His lack of earnings meant that the rent was in arrears, and Mary had resorted to prostitution. This led to arguments between them, and during one particularly heated exchange – apparently when Mary was tipsy – a pane of glass in the window by the door had been broken. The window was now stuffed with newspaper and rags, and was covered by an old coat. Then, in late October, Mary invited a homeless prostitute named Julia to stay with them. This proved too much for Joe Barnet; he decided enough was enough, and moved out.

Maria Harvey, who gave her occupation as 'laundress', told police that she had stayed with Kelly in her room on the Monday and Tuesday nights prior to the murder. She had then taken a room in New Court, Dorset Street, but had spent the Thursday afternoon with Mary Kelly in her room at Miller's Court. At around 7 pm Joe Barnet had arrived and Maria had left, leaving behind her black crepe bonnet, an overcoat, two dirty cotton shirts, a boy's shirt, and a girl's white petticoat.

Joe Barnet had remained on friendly terms with Mary Kelly, and had last seen her alive when he called on her between 7 pm and 8 pm on Thursday November 8th. He later said that there was another woman with them in the room but that she had left first. It is unlikely that he was referring to Maria Harvey, since he knew her and would surely have mentioned her by name. He also said that the woman lived in Miller's Court, which Maria Harvey did not, so he was probably referring to Lizzie Albrook (see below). In his inquest testimony, Barnet stated that he 'last saw her [Mary Kelly] alive between 7:30 and 7:45 the night of Thursday before she was found. I was with her about one hour'. According to Barnet, as he left he told Mary Kelly that he had had no work and was very sorry that he was unable to give her any money. He returned to his lodging house on Bishopsgate and played whist until 12:30 am, at which time he retired to bed.

Lizzie Albrook was 20 years old and a good friend of Kelly's. Her later statements to the press (she was never called as a witness at the inquest) provide a poignant glimpse of Mary Kelly's state of mind on that last night of her life:

About the last thing she said was, 'Whatever you do don't you do wrong and turn out as I have'. She had often spoken to me in this way and warned me against going on the streets as she had done. She told me, too, that she was heartily sick of the life she was leading and wished she had

LEFT: Mary Kelly lived in Dorset Street, which, according to the *Daily Mail*, was the 'worst street in London'.

money enough to go back to Ireland where her people lived. I do not believe she would have gone out as she did if she had not been obliged to do so to keep herself from starvation.

A surprising number of people appear to have met or seen Mary in the hours leading up to her death, and although some witness accounts confuse rather than clarify how she spent the remainder of her last night, the majority help us build up a reasonable picture of her activities into the early hours of Friday November 9th, 1888.

Maurice Lewis, a tailor who lived in Dorset Street, claimed to have known Mary Kelly for five years. He saw her drinking in the Horn of Plenty Pub in Dorset Street with some women, one of whom was named Julia, and a man named Dan who sold oranges at Billingsgate and Spitalfields markets, and with whom she had been living until recently. Evidently he was referring to Joseph Barnet, but was mistaken about his name.

Mary Anne Cox was described in her police statement of November 9th, as being 'a widow and an unfortunate'. She lived at 5 Miller's Court and judging by her comings and goings, she went out soliciting

BELOW: In the early hours of November 9th, 1888, Mary Kelly led her killer through this long-gone archway to the room where her body was discovered later that same day.

ABOVE: Commercial Street showing the Britannia public house to the left and the Ten Bells to the right in the distance. The Britannia stood on the corner of Dorset Street.

several times in the course of the night. Returning to Dorset Street between 11:45 pm and midnight, she saw Mary Jane (the name by which she apparently knew Kelly) walking ahead of her in the company of a man who was carrying a quart can of beer. As Mrs Cox turned into the Court, Mary and the man were entering Kelly's room. Mrs Cox called out, 'Good night, Mary Jane', but Kelly, who was 'very drunk', could scarcely answer, although she did manage to say, 'Good night'.

The man was aged about 36, was 5 feet 5 inches tall, with a fresh complexion and, so she thought, a blotchy face. He had side whiskers, a thick carroty moustache, and was dressed in dark shabby clothes, dark overcoat, and black felt hat. Mrs Cox went to her room and almost immediately heard Mary Kelly singing, 'A violet I plucked from my mother's grave when a boy'. She was still singing when Mrs Cox went out again 15 minutes later, and also when she came back at around 1 am. Having warmed her hands, Mrs Cox went out again and, when she returned at 3 am, Miller's Court was quiet. At Mary Kelly's inquest Mrs Cox testified that she did not go to sleep 'at all', and that she heard 'men going in and out, several go in and out. I heard someone go out at a quarter to six.' However, she didn't know which of the houses he came out of, and she heard no door being shut.

Mrs Elizabeth Prater, who lived in the room above Mary Kelly's, may have heard something even more significant. She had been out for the night and had returned to Miller's Court at around 1 am. According to her police testimony, she stood chatting with John McCarthy, whose chandler's shop was next to the court entrance. At the inquest, however, she told a slightly different tale, claiming that she simply stood outside McCarthy's shop waiting for a man she lived with, and that she spoke with no one. When the man didn't arrive she went up to her room, placed two tables against her door, lay on the bed and having 'had something to drink', slept soundly. At around 3:30 am to 4 am her cat jumped on her, waking her up. As she pushed the cat away, she heard a faint cry of, 'Oh! Murder!' It seemed to come from close by, but since the area was a very violent one and domestic violence was commonplace, she thought it was just another husband abusing his wife. She ignored it, and went back to sleep. She awoke again at 5 am, got up and went over to the Ten Bells pub, arriving at around 5:45 am. She saw a few men harnessing horses in Dorset Street, but nothing suspicious. Having had a drink, she returned to her room and slept soundly till 11 am.

Another witness who may have heard Mary Kelly's last desperate cry for help was Sarah Lewis, a laundress of 24 Great Pearl Street, who passed Christchurch at 2:30 am. She had argued with her husband and decided to spend the rest of the night with her friends Mr and Mrs Keyler, who lived at 2 Miller's Court, a first floor room. According to her police statement, as she approached the court there was a man standing against the lodging house on the opposite side of Dorset Street, although she was unable to describe him. This statement was taken on November 9th, probably in the Keylers' room, as she later testified that the police would not let them out until 5:30 pm. Evidently over the next few days Sarah Lewis gave a lot of thought to this mystery man, and by the time of Mary Kelly's inquest she was able to go into a little more detail:

> He was not tall - but stout - had on a wideawake black hat - I did not notice his clothes - another young man with a woman passed along - The man standing in the street was looking up the court as if waiting for someone to come out.

Her inquest testimony is remarkable for another fact that had, apparently, slipped her mind when making her police statement:

> About Wednesday night at 8 o'clock I was going along Bethnal Green Road with another female and a Gentleman passed us he turned back & spoke to us, he asked us to follow him, and asked one of us he did not mind which, [to go with him] we refused. He went away, and came back & said if we would follow him he would treat us - he asked us to go down a passage - he had a bag he put it down saying what are you frightened of he then undid his coat and felt for something and we ran away - He was short, pale faced, with a black small moustache, about forty years of age - the bag he had was about a foot or nine inches long - he had on a round high hat - he had a brownish long overcoat and a short black coat underneath - and pepper & salt trousers.

> On our running away we did not look after the man - On the Friday morning about half past two when I was coming to Miller's Court I met the same man with a female - in Commercial Street near Mr Ringers Public House - He had then no overcoat on - but he had the bag & the same hat trousers & undercoat.
>
> I passed by them and looked back at the man - I was frightened - I looked again when I got to the corner of Dorset Street. I have not seen the man since I should know him if I did.

The difference between Sarah Lewis's police and inquest testimonies regarding the sinister man she saw on Commercial Street casts some doubt on

LEFT: It was through the broken window pane, visible in this photograph that Thomas Bowyer looked and saw the horribly mutilated body of Mary Kelly.

her veracity as a witness. Her police statement had this to say about him:

> Sarah Lewis further said that when in company with another female on Wednesday evening last at Bethnal Green, a suspicious man accosted her, he carried a bag.

According to the inquest statement, this man had so terrified her and her friend that they had run away. When she saw the same man in the early hours of Friday November 9th, she was frightened once again. Yet it seems that she made no mention of having seen him in Commercial Street when she was interviewed later that day by the police. It is clear that in the days following the murder, Sarah Lewis was filling in the blanks in her memory; by the time she came to give evidence at the inquest, not only had she remembered seeing him, but was also able to give a full description of him:

> He was short, pale faced, with a black small moustache, about forty years of age - the bag he had was about a foot or nine inches long - he had on a round high hat - he had a brownish long overcoat and a short black coat underneath - and pepper & salt trousers.

When her statement is compared to several press stories of meetings with sinister strangers on the day of the murder, surprising similarities occur. The following article, for example, appeared in the *Manchester Guardian* on November 10th, two days before Mary Kelly's inquest:

> Mrs Paumier, a chestnut seller at the corner of Widcoate-street, a narrow thoroughfare about two minutes' walk from the scene of the murder, told a reporter a story which appear (sic) to afford a clue to the murder. She said that about 12 o'clock this morning a man dressed like a gentleman came to her and said, 'I suppose you have heard about the murder in Dorset-street'. She replied that she had, whereupon the man grinned and said 'I know more about it than you'. He then stared into her face and went down Sandys Row, another narrow thoroughfare which cuts across Widcoate-street. When he had got some way off he looked back, as if to see whether she was watching him, and then vanished. Mrs Paumier said the man had a black moustache, was about 5ft. 6in. in height, and wore a black silk hat, black coat, and speckled trousers. He carried a black bag about 1ft. in depth and 1½ ft. in length. Sarah Roney, a girl about 20 years of age, states that she was with two other girls last night in Brushfield-street, which is near Dorset-street, when a man wearing a tall hat and a black coat, and carrying a black bag, came up to her, and said, 'Will you come with me?' She told him she would not, and asked him what he had in the bag, and he said, 'Something the ladies don't like'. He then walked away.

Evidently, rumoured sightings of the villain (and if you read the descriptions again, you will see that he bore an uncanny resemblance to the traditional Victorian villain as portrayed on stage and in pantomime and film) were circulating in the area by the Saturday. It is possible that Sarah Lewis was influenced more by these 'rumours' than by what she actually saw and that, for some reason, she transported the man who had frightened her on Bethnal Green Road to Commercial Street on the morning of the murder.

When Sarah Lewis arrived at the Keylers' room, she sat in a chair and dozed for a while. She woke up at about 3:30 am. A little before 4 am, she heard a female voice shout loudly, 'Murder!' The sound seemed to come from the direction of Mary Kelly's room, but since there was only one scream, Sarah ignored it.

Since the man that she saw leaning against the lodging house wall appears in both her statements, it seems reasonable to assume that this section of her testimony was reliable. His identity was possibly revealed on

The scene of the murder, Miller's Court.

The awful discovery by McCarthy.

The seventh victim picked out for slaughter from descriptions g[iven]

Startling story of a man with a black bag

ABOVE: John McCarthy, Mary Kelly's landlord, would later describe the sight he saw through her window as being 'more like the work of a devil than of a man.'

the following Monday, when at 6 pm a man named George Hutchinson, who lived at the Victoria Home on Commercial Street, walked into Commercial Street Police Station to tell of an encounter he had had with Mary Kelly at around 2 am on the morning of her murder. He claimed that he had known her for three years and said that he had occasionally given her a few shillings. In his statement, which was taken down by Inspector Abberline, he told how:

About 2 am on the 9th I was coming by Thrawl Street, Commercial Street and just before I got to Flower and Dean Street I met the murdered woman Kelly and she said to me: 'Hutchinson, will you lend me sixpence?' I said: 'I can't. I have spent all my money going down to Romford.' She said: 'Good morning, I must go and find some money'. She went away to Thrawl Street. A man coming in the opposite direction to Kelly (i.e. from Aldgate) tapped her on the shoulder and said something to her. They both burst out laughing. I heard her say: 'All right' to him and the man said: 'You will be alright for what I have told you'. He then placed his right hand around her shoulder. He also had a kind of small parcel in his left hand with a kind of strap around it. I stood against the lamp of the Queen's Head Public House and watched him. They both came past me and the man hung his head down with his hat over his eyes. I stooped down and looked him in the face. He looked at me stern. They both went into Dorset Street. I followed them. They both stood on the corner of the court for about three minutes. He said something to her. She said: 'All right, my dear. Come along. You will be comfortable.' He then placed his arm on her shoulder and she gave him a kiss. She said she had lost her handkerchief. He then pulled out his handkerchief, a red one, and gave it to her. They both went up the court together. I went to the court to see if I could see them, but I could not. I stood there for about three quarters of an hour to see if they came out. They did not, so I went away.

Hutchinson then proceeded to give an incredibly detailed description of the man:

Age about thirty four or thirty five; height five feet six inches; complexion pale; dark eyes and eyelashes; slight moustache curled up at each end and hair dark; very surly looking; dress - long dark coat; collar and cuffs trimmed with astrakhan and a dark jacket underneath; light waistcoat; dark trousers; dark felt hat turned down in the middle; button boots and gaiters with white buttons; wore a very thick gold chain with linen collar; black tie with horseshoe pin; respectable appearance; walked very sharp; Jewish appearance. Can be identified.

Abberline took Hutchinson's statement very seriously and assigned him two detectives who spent two days escorting him around the area in the hope that he might see the man again and identify him. Today Hutchinson's statement arouses a good deal of debate. Many argue that he could not have witnessed all that he claimed to have seen, and it has been pointed out that his description of the man sounds too good to be true. When compared to sightings by other witnesses this becomes very evident. But what possible reason could Hutchinson have had for volunteering a false statement that actually placed him at the scene of Mary Kelly's murder? It has been argued that he was just another publicity seeker, anxious to involve himself in the flurry of speculation that followed the murder. If so he was playing a dangerous game by placing himself so close to the crime scene and admitting to keeping the victim under surveillance. Another possible scenario is that Hutchinson knew he had been spotted, panicked, and spent the next few days honing an alibi to explain his proximity to the murder site. This of course would explain why he waited two days to come forward and why his description was so detailed compared to those of other witnesses. In recent years, Hutchinson's name has even found its way onto the ever-expanding list of Jack the Ripper suspects.

Today, it is almost impossible to ascertain the reliability of Hutchinson's statement. Given that he did not appear as a witness at Mary Kelly's inquest, he was neither cross-examined by the coroner nor questioned by the jury, so his statement was never subjected to the scrutiny that may have proved or disproved it once and for all. The problem with dismissing him outright is that Abberline, an experienced and intelligent detective, gave it as his opinion that Hutchison's statement was true. So he must remain one of several unexplained mysteries concerning the final hours of Mary Kelly's life.

One of the major mysteries concerning the murder of Mary Kelly is when exactly it took place. Dr. Thomas Bond, the police divisional surgeon who together with Dr. Phillips examined Mary Kelly's body in situ, estimated that she had been murdered some time between 1 am and 2 am. Dr. Phillips placed the time of death at around 4 am. This latter time would be in keeping with the cry of 'Murder!' that Elizabeth Prater and Sarah Lewis claim to have heard. Yet sightings of Mary Kelly continued long after this hour.

Mrs Caroline Maxwell, wife of Henry Maxwell, a lodging house deputy at 14 Dorset Street, claimed that she saw Mary Kelly standing at the corner of Miller's Court between 8 am and 8:30 am.

'What brings you up so early?' Mrs Maxwell asked.

'Oh! I do feel so bad', was Mary Kelly's reply. 'I have the horrors of drink upon me, as I have been drinking for some days past.'

Mrs Maxwell suggested she should go to Mrs Ringers [the Britannia pub] and have half a pint of beer. Mary told her that she had already done so, but had brought it all up again, and so saying pointed to some vomit in the roadway. Caroline Maxwell then headed to Bishopsgate on an errand, and when she returned at around 9 am she saw Mary standing outside the Britannia talking to a man. Although she was some distance away from them, she thought the man was aged about 30, that he was around 5 feet 5 inches tall, of stout build, and that he was dressed as a market porter.

Mrs Maxwell's statement is clearly at odds with both Bond's and Phillips' opinion regarding the time of death. And if Sarah Lewis and Elizabeth Prater did hear Mary cry out as she was being murdered at around

4 am, how could Mrs Maxwell have seen her twice between 8 am and 9 am? There are many theories about these sightings. Some hold that Caroline Maxwell was mistaken about the day, or that she was lying because she wanted her moment in the spotlight. Others argue that she mistook someone else for Mary Kelly (she did say that she had only actually spoken to Kelly twice). Inevitably it has been proffered that she saw Mary's ghost, while conspiracy theorists argue that she did in fact meet Mary Kelly, and that the body in the room was that of someone else.

Yet Caroline Maxwell's account of the meeting is consistent in both her police statement and her inquest testimony. Furthermore, the coroner at the inquest made a specific point of warning her that she was giving evidence under oath, and pointed out that her testimony contradicted those of other witnesses. But Caroline Maxwell stuck to her story. Evidently she was convinced she had met Mary Kelly, not someone who looked like her or was dressed in her clothes, at 8 am on the morning of her murder. On November 12th, *The Times* went so far as to report that at least part of Caroline Maxwell's story had been corroborated:

> When asked by the police how she could fix the time of the morning, Mrs Maxwell replied, 'Because I went to the milkshop for some milk, and I had not before been there for a long time, and that she was wearing a woollen cross-over that I had not seen her wear for a considerable time'. On inquiries being made at the milkshop indicated by the woman her statement was found to be correct, and the cross-over was also found in Kelly's room.

So we find ourselves confronted by another inexplicable mystery concerning the murder of Mary Kelly. Caroline Maxwell appears to have been a reliable and consistent witness, and part of her story was corroborated by staff at the milkshop. Given that Mary Kelly's body had been virtually skinned to the bone, and that the window to her room was broken, the room temperature would have been extremely cold; the body would have cooled a lot more rapidly than normal. And so the possibility remains that the doctors were wrong about the time of her death. Caroline Maxwell may, therefore, have met Mary Kelly just as she described, and the man she saw with her could have been her murderer.

At 10:45 am on November 9th Mary Kelly's landlord, John McCarthy, sent his assistant Thomas Bowyer (also known as Indian Harry) round to 13 Miller's Court to collect her overdue rent. Striding into Miller's Court, Bowyer banged twice on her door. There was no answer. No doubt believing that she was inside but unwilling or unable to pay her rent, Bowyer stepped around the corner and pulled aside a curtain that covered the broken window pane. Moments later an ashen-faced Bowyer staggered back into McCarthy's shop.

'Governor', he spluttered, 'I knocked at the door and could not make anyone answer. I looked through the window and saw a lot of blood'.

'You don't mean that, Harry', was McCarthy's horrified response, and the two men hurried from the shop and into Miller's Court.

Stooping down, McCarthy pushed aside the curtain and peered into the gloomy room. A sight of unimaginable horror met his eyes. The wall behind the bed was spattered with blood. On the bedside table was a pile of bloody human flesh. And there on the bed, barely recognizable as human, lay the virtually skinned-down cadaver of Mary Kelly.

McCarthy sent Bowyer to Commercial Street Police Station for the police; then, securing his shop, he hurried after him. Inspectors Walter Dew and Walter Beck were at the station when Bowyer arrived.

As Dew recalled in his memoirs, 'The poor fellow was so frightened that for a time he was unable to utter a single intelligible word. At last he managed to stammer out something about 'Another one. Jack the Ripper. Awful. Jack McCarthy sent me".'

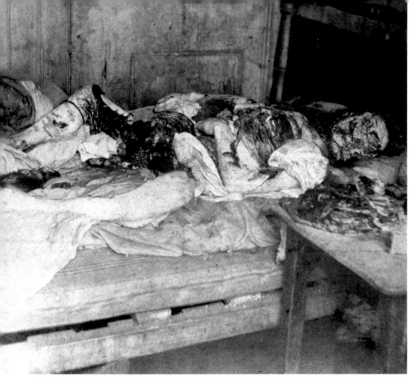

Soon Beck and Dew were following Bowyer along Commercial Street in the direction of Dorset Street. When they arrived at Miller's Court, Dew tried the door but it would not open. Inspector Beck therefore moved to the window and gazed into the room.

Almost instantly he staggered back. 'For God's sake, Dew,' he cried, 'don't look'.

Dew ignored the order and looked through the window. He then saw a sight that would stay with him to his dying day. The horror of what he saw was still vivid in his mind when he penned his memoirs 50 years on:

> As my thoughts go back to Miller's Court, and what happened there, the old nausea, indignation and horror overwhelm me still... My mental picture of it remains as shockingly clear as though it were but yesterday... No savage could have been more barbaric. No wild animal could have done anything so horrifying.

Mary Kelly's body lay on the bed, her head turned towards the window. Her face had been mutilated beyond recognition and one feature in particular struck Inspector Dew: 'The poor woman's eyes. They were wide open, and seemed to be staring straight at me with a look of terror.'

Indeed, so horrific were the mutilations to Mary Kelly's face that her lover Joseph Barnet was later only able to identify her by her eyes and ears.

Dr. George Bagster Phillips arrived at 11:15 am and Inspector Abberline was at the scene 15 minutes later.

Dr. Phillips suggested that no one should enter the room until bloodhounds had been brought to the scene and put on the scent. As they waited, the police sealed off both ends of Dorset Street and the entrance to Miller's Court was closed.

At 1:30 pm Inspector Arnold, the head of H Division, arrived and announced that the bloodhounds would not be coming after all, and gave instructions for the door to be forced open. John McCarthy fetched a pickax and proceeded to batter it down. The scene inside the room was one of utter, bloody carnage. No doubt John McCarthy was expressing the sentiments of all those present when he later told a journalist:

> The sight that we saw I cannot drive away from my mind. It looked more like the work of a devil than of a man. I had heard a great deal about the Whitechapel murders, but I declare to God I had never expected to see such a sight as this. The whole scene is more than I can describe. I hope I may never see such a sight as this again.

Dr. Thomas Bond, who arrived in the room at 2 pm and carried out an examination of the body with Dr.

Phillips, detailed Mary Kelly's horrendous injuries in his subsequent post mortem report. Even today, inured as we are by graphic depictions of violence and bloodshed across the media, the detached scientific tone of his report makes for disturbing reading:

> The body was lying naked in the middle of the bed, the shoulders flat, but the axis of the body inclined to the left side of the bed. The head was turned on the left cheek. The left arm was close to the body with the forearm flexed at a right angle & lying across the abdomen. The right arm was slightly abducted from the body & rested on the mattress, the elbow bent & the forearm supine with the fingers clenched. The legs were wide apart, the left thigh at right angles to the trunk & the right forming an obtuse angle with the pubes.
>
> The whole of the surface of the abdomen & thighs was removed & the abdominal Cavity emptied of its viscera. The breasts were cut off, the arms mutilated by several jagged wounds & the face hacked beyond recognition of the features. The tissues of the neck were severed all round down to the bone.
>
> The viscera were found in various parts viz: the uterus & Kidneys with one breast under the head, the other breast by the Rt foot, the Liver between the feet, the intestines by the right side & the spleen by the left side of the body. The flaps removed from the abdomen and thighs were on a table.
>
> The bed clothing at the right corner was saturated with blood, & on the floor beneath was a pool of blood covering about 2 feet square. The wall by the right side of the bed & in a line with the neck was marked by blood which had struck it in a number of separate splashes.
>
> The face was gashed in all directions the nose cheeks, eyebrows and ears being partly removed. The lips were blanched & cut by several incisions running obliquely down to the chin. There were also numerous cuts extending irregularly across all the features.

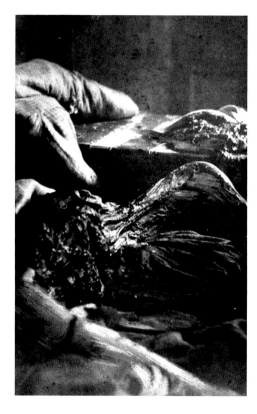

As the doctors went about their grim task, the police began examining the room itself. There had been a fierce fire in the grate, the heat from which had been so intense that it had melted the handle and spout of the kettle. In the ashes, the police discovered the charred wire rim of a woman's hat, indicating that the fuel for the fire had been provided by the clothes Maria Harvey had left in Mary Kelly's room. Inspector Abberline was of the opinion that the murderer had burnt the clothing to provide sufficient light for him to work by. Mary Kelly's clothes were found on a chair at the foot of the bed.

By 3:45 pm the doctors had completed their examination. Instructions were given for the removal of Mary Kelly's body to the mortuary. *The Times* reported:

> At 10 minutes to 4 o'clock a one-horse carrier's cart, with the ordinary tarpaulin cover was driven into Dorset-street, and halted opposite Millers-court. From the cart was taken a long shell or coffin, dirty and scratched with constant use. This was taken

RIGHT: Another photograph of Mary Kelly, looking over her leg and abdomen, towards the bedside table.

into the death chamber, and there the remains were temporarily coffined. The news that the body was about to be removed caused a great rush of people from the courts running out of Dorset-street, and there was a determined effort to break the police cordon at the Commercial-street end. The crowd, which pressed round the van, was of the humblest class, but the demeanour of the poor people was all that could be described. Ragged caps were doffed and slatternly-looking women shed tears as the shell, covered with a ragged-looking cloth, was placed in the van.

Meanwhile the police went about their by now familiar routine of interviewing witnesses and hunting for suspects. Sergeant Thicke and several other officers began taking down statements from those who lived in the immediate vicinity and took full particulars of people staying at the common lodging houses in Dorset Street. Something of the magnitude of their task can be gleaned from press comments 'that in one house alone there are upwards of 260 persons, and that several houses accommodate over 200'.

The day was to hold another shock for the beleaguered officers, for word came through that their commissioner, Sir Charles Warren, had resigned. The reason for his resignation was more to do with the strained relations between himself and the home secretary, Henry Matthews, than with his force's inability to catch Jack the Ripper. Warren had responded to press attacks on the police with an article that was published in *Murray's Magazine* entitled 'The Police of the Metropolis'. This was in direct contravention of official procedure, which required that all articles should first be cleared by senior Home Office officials. Matthews sent him a stern reprimand for his impropriety and Warren responded by tendering his resignation. Although the formalities had been under way for a few days, his resignation was officially accepted and announced on the day of Mary Kelly's murder. Warren actually remained in office until a new commissioner was appointed, and gave several orders for the handling of the Mary Kelly investigation. His reign as commissioner ended on November 27th when he was replaced by the former subordinate with whom he had clashed at the end of August, James Monro.

As darkness fell on November 9th, the police nailed boards over the windows of Mary Kelly's room and padlocked the door shut. A strange silence descended over Dorset Street as the residents attempted to comprehend the horror of what had occurred in their midst.

The week that followed Mary Kelly's murder saw an intense flurry of activity. A hasty inquest was held on Monday November 12th and was brought to a close that same day, probably at the request of the police, in order to starve the press of the gossip and gory detail of which they had made so much during the protracted inquests into the previous murders. The number of plain clothes officers in the area was increased from 89 to 143, and these men patrolled the streets of Whitechapel after nightfall. Meanwhile the Home Office authorized Sir Charles Warren to issue a notice offering a pardon to any accomplice who would give information that would lead to the discovery and conviction of the killer. And the fresh panic that was now gripping the capital even snapped the patience of Queen Victoria, who fired off an angry missive to her Prime Minister, Lord Salisbury:

This new most ghastly murder shows the absolute necessity for some very decided action. All these courts must be lit, & our detectives improved. They are not what they should be.

At noon on Monday November 19th, the bell at St Leonard's church in Shoreditch began to toll a mourning knell as a coffin of elm and oak, borne on the shoulders of four men, was carried out of the gates in front of a crowd some several thousand strong. Men and women alike could barely control their emotions as the funeral procession set off for St Patrick's Roman Catholic Cemetery in Leyton. It was with great difficulty that the police forced a path for the cortege as onlookers jostled to touch the coffin and read its simple brass plate: Marie Jeanette Kelly, died 9th November 1888, aged twenty five years.

What nobody could have realized as Mary Kelly was laid to rest was that in Miller's Court, Jack the Ripper had performed his swansong. That knowledge would only come with hindsight. Over the weeks that followed, the panic and fear that had gripped the neighborhood throughout the autumn began to abate as the residents returned to their everyday struggle for survival, and the press began to focus on other matters.

The police pursued their inquiries well into the winter and continued to arrest suspect after suspect, but to no avail; one by one, the arrestees were absolved of any hand in the crimes. The plainclothes amateur patrols continued plodding the streets after dark, but by February 1889 even they had begun to tire of the seemingly endless hours and harsh weather conditions. Gradually, they began to disband. On January 26th, 1889 the new Metropolitan Police Commissioner, James Monro, informed the Home Office that he was going to start reducing the number of plainclothes police officers 'as quickly as it is safe to do so'. He cut the number from 143 to 102 at once, and cut them again in February to 47. Thereafter they were phased out altogether. Two further murders, that of Alice McKenzie in the early hours of July 17th, 1889 and that of Frances Coles on February 13th, 1891 raised the chilling possibility that the killer had returned, but these are generally not considered to have been the work of Jack the Ripper. As he walked away from Miller's Court, the Whitechapel murderer left behind him one of the most enduring mysteries in history, and the legend of Jack the Ripper would grow in stature with every subsequent year that passed.

Today people travel from all over the world to tour the murder sites and walk through the streets of Whitechapel. Some of those streets are still as sordid and down at heel as they were in 1888. Others have seen significant gentrification, and what were once slum dwellings have become very desirable and expensive properties. The Ten Bells pub, where Mary Kelly spent some of the last hours of her short life, is still going strong, although it is trying to distance itself as much as possible from its past association with the Ripper. In the nearby Princess Alice, opposite which Leather Apron was said to have once threatened the prostitutes of the area, the Whitechapel Society meets regularly to discuss the murders and exchange Jack the Ripper gossip and memorabilia over a pint or two. The Frying Pan Pub, where Mary Nichols drank away her doss money shortly before being murdered, has now become the Sheraz Indian Restaurant. The doorway in Goulston Street where the piece of Catherine Eddowe's apron was found is now the takeaway counter of a fish and chip shop. People still make their way out to St Patrick's Roman Catholic Cemetery in Leyton to lay flowers on the grave of Mary Kelly and spend a few moments in quiet contemplation.

In 2006, Jack the Ripper was voted the worst Briton ever, even though we don't know who he was, nor even if he was actually British. But there is an intriguing paradox on which to end our journey into Jack the Ripper's London. For the names of his five victims—Mary Nichols, Annie Chapman, Elizabeth Stride, Catherine Eddowes, and Mary Kelly—would not be remembered today had it not been for the fact that they were murdered by a man whose name will probably never be known for sure.

RIGHT: People still lay flowers on the grave of Mary Kelly, the final victim of Jack the Ripper.

IN LOVING MEMORY OF
MARIE JEANETTE KELLY
NONE BUT THE LONELY HEARTS
CAN KNOW MY SADNESS
LOVE LIVES FOREVER.

FURTHER READING

Begg, Paul. *Jack the Ripper: The Definitive History*. Pearson Education, 2003

Begg, Paul. *Jack the Ripper: The Facts*. Robson Books, 2004

Begg, Paul et al. *The Jack the Ripper A–Z*. Headline, 1996

Braund, Nathan and Jakubowski, Maxim. *The Mammoth Book of Jack the Ripper*. Robinson Publishing, 1999

Chesney, Kellow. *The Victorian Underworld*. Penguin, 1989

Curtis, L. Perry. *Jack the Ripper and the London Press*. Yale University Press, 2001

Eddleston, John J.. *Jack the Ripper Encyclopaedia*. Metro, 2002

Evans, Stewart P. and Skinner, Keith. *The Ultimate Jack the Ripper Sourcebook*. Robinson, 2001

Evans, Stewart P. and Skinner Keith. *Jack the Ripper. Letters From Hell*. Sutton Publishing, 2001

Fido, Martin. The Crimes, Detection and Death of Jack the Ripper. Weidenfeld and Nicholson, 1987

Fishman, William J.. *The Streets of East London*. Duckworth, 1989

Fishman, William J.. *East End 1888*. Five Leaves Publications, 1988

Fried, Albert and Elman, Richard M. (Editors). *Charles Booth's London*. Penguin, 1969

Jones, Richard. *Walking Dickensian London*. New Holland, 2004

Koven, Seth. Slumming: *Sexual and Social Politics in Victorian London*. Princeton University Press, 2004

London, Jack. *The People of the Abyss*. The Journeyman Press, 1992

Ryder, Stephen P.. *Public Reactions to Jack the Ripper*. Dan Norder, Inklings Press, 2006

Scott, Christopher. *Will the Real Mary Kelly…?* Publish and Be Damned, 2005

Sugden, Philip. *The Complete History of Jack the Ripper*. Robinson, 2002

Walkowitz, Judith R.. *City of Dreadful Delight*. The University of Chicago Press, 1992

Walkowitz, Judith R.. *Prostitution and Victorian Society*. Cambridge University Press, 1982

INDEX

Page references in *italics* indicate illustrations

ACKNOWLEDGEMENTS

So many people helped with the research and writing of this book. The staff at both the Guildhall Library and Tower Hamlets Local Studies Library were totally supportive in helping me dig out nuggets of information. My old friend Paul Begg was willing to listen to my theories and provided encouragement throughout the project. Lindsay Siviter, whose research skills and knowledge on the subject deserve a much wider airing, provided many useful insights. I'd like to say a huge thank you to Stephen P. Ryder, whose Internet resource, www.casebook.org, has made so much information available to such a wide audience. Many thanks also to Alan McCormick, the curator of the Metropolitan Police's Crime Museum and to Roger Appleby of the City of London Police Museum. Jeff Leahy made some great suggestions, all of which were much appreciated. I'd like to thank Sean East for his photography, and also the Canary Wharf Group for their kind assistance in obtaining photographs of East London. On a personal note, I'd like to thank my sister Geraldine Hennigan for being ever willing to listen and offer advice. As always my wife, Joanne, was supportive and understanding. My sons Thomas and William provided a great deal of light relief, particularly in telling their teachers that their dad was Jack the Ripper. I'd like to thank New Holland Publishers for the chance to write this book. Finally I'd like to pay my respects to Mary Nichols, Annie Chapman, Elizabeth Stride, Catherine Eddowes, and Mary Kelly. May you all rest in peace.

PHOTO ACKNOWLEDGEMENTS

All photographs taken by Sean East, except for those credited below:

New Holland Publishers (UK) Ltd: pages 10, 11,13, 16, 21, 32, 61, 68, 71, 76, 77, 82, 96, 109, 110, 117
Tower Hamlets Local History Library and Archives: pages 12, 33, 40, 43, 55, 58, 75, 81
Richard Jones: pages 19, 23, 49, 54, 57, 59, 63, 66, 88, 90, 92, 99, 107, 112, 113, 115
Guildhall Library, Corporation of London: page 31
Mr J. Connor: page 40